SELECTED PAPERS OF
GREAT AMERICAN PHYSICISTS

SPENCER R. WEART, *editor*

Editorial Board: WILLIAM FOWLER,

W.W. HAVENS, JR., MARTIN KLEIN,

ROBERT SHANKLAND, CHIEN-SHIUNG WU

SELECTED PAPERS OF

PAPERS OF

GREAT

AMERICAN

PHYSICISTS

The Bicentennial Commemorative Volume of The American Physical Society 1976

AMERICAN INSTITUTE OF PHYSICS

NEW YORK

Cover illustration:
Franklin's Leyden jar.

L.C. Catalog Card No. 76-2991
ISBN 0-88318-224-6

Published for The American
Physical Society by the
American Institute of Physics
335 East 45th Street
New York, N.Y. 10017

Designed by Philip Grushkin

Printed in the United States of America

Contents

Preface *by William A. Fowler*   7

BENJAMIN FRANKLIN   *10*

Letter IV: Farther Experiments and Observations
   in Electricity   *15*

Letter XI   *33*

JOSEPH HENRY   *35*

On the Production of Currents and Sparks of
   Electricity from Magnetism   *40*

On Electro-Dynamic Induction *(extract)*   *46*

ALBERT ABRAHAM MICHELSON   *63*

On the Relative Motion of the Earth and the
   Luminiferous Ether *(with Edward W. Morley)*   *68*

HENRY AUGUSTUS ROWLAND   *81*

Screw   *85*

The Highest Aim of the Physicist   *91*

JOSIAH WILLARD GIBBS   *104*

Preface to *Elementary Principles in
Statistical Mechanics*   *109*

ROBERT ANDREWS MILLIKAN 115
On the Elementary Electrical Charge and the
Avogadro Constant *(extract)* 120

ARTHUR HOLLY COMPTON 148
A Quantum Theory of the Scattering of X-Rays
by Light Elements 152

Afterword: The Last Fifty Years 173
Sources 176

CONTENTS

Preface

American physics is second to none in the world. It was not always so. This volume, issued by The American Physical Society to celebrate the American Bicentennial, contains representative and readable selections of the papers of great American physicists which illustrate the rise of American physics from colonial days through the early years of the twentieth century. This is primarily a commemorative volume with no scholarly pretensions other than fidelity to the original form in which physicists saw the works of their contemporaries. In these reproductions of original papers we are brought closer to the past of our profession and our country.

The roll call is impressive, Franklin, Henry, Gibbs, Rowland, Michelson, Millikan, Compton; a signer of the Declaration of Independence and first great American physicist, a founder and second President of the National Academy of Sciences, the first great American theoretical physicist, the first President of The American Physical Society and the first three American Nobel Prize winners in Physics. The selections stop short of the last fifty years since choices involving living people and their deceased colleagues are difficult to make.

Many American physicists, including all whose papers appear in this volume, studied in Europe or benefited from close personal contacts with European colleagues. In this and many other ways, American physics owes a great debt to the old countries. In providing sanctuary in time of war and strife to many physicists from these and other countries, America has repaid its debt. Most important of all, American physicists join with their colleagues throughout the world in the support of free and untrammeled research and teaching and the advocacy of uncensored international exchange of new knowledge in physics and other sciences.

The important role played by applied physics, or "practical" physics in earlier terminology, is a central theme in the early research. Franklin's work on lightning led him immediately to invent and study the

7

lightning rod, while Henry helped put his own discoveries to work. Meanwhile research in pure physics gradually attained adequate support in America; never have more pithy arguments for intellectual enterprise *per se* been put forward than in Rowland's "The Highest Aim of the Physicist".

Practicality and pure research were leavened, then as now, by good humor. There is fascination and delight in Franklin's "magical picture of the KING (God preserve him)" and hilarity in his description of the electric "party of pleasure on the banks of the *Skuylkil*." That physics is fun is not a new discovery of our more ebullient contemporaries — Henry devotes a paragraph in his article "On Electro-Dynamic Induction", reproduced here, to *physique amusante*, albeit with some apology and reticence. It is hoped that others, and young people in particular, will come to share with those of us in physics the fascination, delight and fun of our profession as well as its intellectual satisfaction and practical contributions.

Our knowledge of the physical world is the result of the efforts of many physicists, not just that of the great physicists. It might have been appropriate to select an important paper by a relatively unsung physicist, but this has not been done. We are human in paying our homage primarily to our heroes. Even so there is great satisfaction in knowing that the selected papers in this volume rest on the foundation of the work of many like ourselves.

The American Physical Society has played a growing role in the affairs of physics over the last 77 years. Its traditional function of holding meetings and publishing journals has been augmented in recent years by an increasing involvement in relating physics to public affairs. This involvement will continue to grow during the third century of the Republic. In this Bicentennial year we look back with pride and some nostalgia to the work of our predecessors and at the same time we look forward to the future of our profession as both an intellectual enterprise for the individual and as a practical enterprise for society.

William A. Fowler
President
The American Physical Society

SELECTED PAPERS OF
GREAT AMERICAN PHYSICISTS

BENJAMIN FRANKLIN

1706-1790

In 1776 Benjamin Franklin helped draft the Declaration of Independence and soon after set sail for Paris, sent by the Continental Congress to negotiate a treaty with the French. He was welcomed with great enthusiasm, for his fame had preceded him—fame not as a statesman but as a scientist. He was already one of the eight foreign associates of the French Academy of Sciences (a century would pass before another American got this rare honor). As the "Newton of electricity" whose theories, experiments and lightning rods were known the length of Europe, Franklin was given a respectful hearing. Deliberately simple in dress and manner, sparkling with wit and homely wisdom, Franklin quickly convinced his audience that he—and by extension the newborn United States of America—embodied unspoiled virtue. He became perhaps the chief factor in winning the support of the French government and its fleet, support which proved decisive in the War for Independence. If Franklin the diplomat could achieve so much, it was largely because first he was Franklin the scientist.

He was forty years old before he took up scientific research; until then he had been chiefly concerned with earning a living. His brief formal education ended at the age of ten when he was removed from school to help his father, a Boston chandler and soapmaker. But he had acquired an interest in books and was soon apprenticed to his elder brother, a printer. Before the end of his apprenticeship he ran away to seek his fortune, and after a short time in Philadelphia, sailed for England. In London he perfected his knowledge of the art of printing and made friends with some gentlemen scientists. He just missed being introduced to the aging Isaac Newton. Returning to Philadelphia in 1726, Franklin set up a printing business. His *Poor Richard's Almanack* and other publications were popular, and he also succeeded in colonial society, throwing himself enthusiastically into every variety of civic affairs.

In 1743 an itinerant lecturer from England demonstrated the latest electrical experiments to the wondering colonials. Franklin saw these demonstrations and later bought the lecturer's entire apparatus. In 1745 he began to experiment on his own, and soon after turned the management of his printing business over to a partner. "When I disengaged myself ... from private business," he wrote, "I flatter'd myself that, by the sufficient tho' modest fortune I had acquired, I had secured leisure during the rest of my life for philosophical studies and amusements."

Experimental "philosophy" and parlor "amusements" were not far apart in the 1740's. The phenomena of electricity in particular seemed of minor importance; often they were studied out of simple fascination with the curious toys and perplexing contradictions that made up the bulk of the subject. Franklin, too, invented such tricks: see the queer game of "treason" and the electrical barbecue in Letter IV, below. But he also sought the principles behind the games. Aided by Philadelphia friends, but using chiefly his own skilled hands and ingenious brain, he devised simple — sometimes overly simple — explanations for the bewildering variety of electrical phenomena. (During the same period he also served on the Philadelphia city council and the Pennsylvania assembly, and was much occupied with the problem of defending the colony from hostile Indians and privateers.)

Electricity, said Franklin, is a substance which is conserved, and which may be either "positive" (in excess) or "negative" (deficient) in a body. The electrical fluid or "fire" repels itself and is attracted to the substratum of "common matter." Franklin also held that the common matter attracts itself; it was left to one of his admirers, Franz Æpinus, to show that Franklin's principles required that common matter repels itself. Despite its flaws, the "Franklinist" theory explained electrical phenomena far better than any previous one, and after improvement by Æpinus and others it drove its rivals from the field throughout Europe.

Franklin meanwhile proposed an experiment which would prove at the same time two exciting conjectures: that electricity is a powerful and universal force of nature, and that this force can be controlled. He suggested that a sharp point might "draw" electricity from a thundercloud, just as a grounded point will discharge a nearby charged object in the laboratory. This "Philadelphia experiment" was first tried in France with a tall pointed rod; it worked, making Franklin famous as the man who showed how to steal sparks from the lightning. A little later and independently he tried the experiment himself, using a kite instead of a tall rod.

While his electrical work was his greatest scientific achievement, Franklin also contributed to knowledge of heat conduction, storms, the Gulf Stream, etc., and invented bifocal glasses, the rocking chair, daylight saving time, and more. He might have done more still, but after he had been working for only a few years on electricity, his country called him to other tasks. He put aside his researches reluctantly and even into his old age kept hoping to return to them.

Franklin's discoveries were reported in his letters to his English friend Peter Collinson and were published in London in a book, from which the selections below are drawn. The results in Letter IV may seem commonplace to a modern physicist where they are not simply confused, but in fact most of this communication was new, startling and highly significant. A few words of explanation may help. The letter deals with a Leyden jar or *phial* filled with water connected to a terminal or *hook* and coated with conducting foil connected to a wire or *tail*. Also used are *electrics*, which we would now call dielectrics, such as glass or wax; a *non-electric* is a conductor. The letter contains the first statement of the Law of Conservation of Charge, the first useful theory of the action of a condenser, and much else. We also give an excerpt reporting the kite experiment.

EXPERIMENTS

AND

OBSERVATIONS

ON

ELECTRICITY,

MADE AT

PHILADELPHIA in AMERICA,

BY

BENJAMIN FRANKLIN, L. L. D. and F. R. S.

To which are added,

LETTERS and PAPERS

ON

PHILOSOPHICAL SUBJECTS.

The Whole corrected, methodized, improved, and now first collected into one Volume,

AND

Illustrated with COPPER PLATES.

———

LONDON:

Printed for DAVID HENRY ; and sold by FRANCIS NEWBERY, at the Corner of St. Paul's Church-Yard.

MDCCLXIX.

LETTER IV.

FROM

BENJ. FRANKLIN, *Esq*; in *Philadelphia*,

TO

PETER COLLINSON, Esq; F.R.S. *London*.

Farther EXPERIMENTS *and* OBSERVATIONS *in*
ELECTRICITY.

SIR,   1748.

§ 1. THERE will be the fame explofion and fhock if the electrified phial is held in one hand by the hook, and the coating touch'd with the other, as when held by the coating, and touch'd at the hook.

2. To

2. To take the charg'd phial fafely by the hook, and not at the fame time diminifh its force, it muft firft be fet down on an electric *per fe*.

3. The phial will be electrified as ftrongly, if held by the hook, and the coating apply'd to the globe or tube ; as when held by the coating, and the hook apply'd *.

4. But the *direction* of the electrical fire being different in the charging, will alfo be different in the explofion. The bottle charged through the hook, will be difcharged through the hook ; the bottle charged through the coating, will be difcharged through the coating, and not otherways ; for the fire muft come out the fame way it went in.

5. To prove this, take two bottles that were equally charged through the hooks, one in each hand : bring their hooks near each other, and no fpark or fhock will follow ; becaufe each hook is difpofed to give fire, and neither to receive it. Set one of the bottles down on glafs, take it up by the hook, and apply its coating to the hook of the other ; then there will be an explofion and fhock, and both bottles will be difcharged.

6. Vary the experiment, by charging two phials equally, one through the hook, the other through the coating : hold that by the coating which was charged through the hook ; and that by the hook which was charged through the coating : apply the hook of the firft to the coating of the

* This was a Difcovery of the very ingenious Mr *Kinnerfley*'s, and by him communicated to me.

other,

other, and there will be no fhock or fpark. Set that down on glafs which you held by the hook, take it up by the coating, and bring the two hooks together: a fpark and fhock will follow, and both phials be difcharged.

In this experiment the bottles are totally difcharged, or the equilibrium within them reftored. The *abounding* of fire in one of the hooks (or rather in the internal furface of one bottle (being exactly equal to the *wanting* of the other: and therefore, as each bottle has in itfelf the *abounding* as well as the *wanting*, the wanting and abounding muft be equal in each bottle. See §. 8, 9, 10, 11. But if a man holds in his hands two bottles, one fully electrified, the other not at all, and brings their hooks together, he has but half a fhock, and the bottles will both remain half electrified, the one being half difcharged, and the other half charged.

7. Place two phials equally charged on a table at five or fix inches diftance. Let a cork-ball, fufpended by a filk thread, hang between them. If the phials were both charged through their hooks, the cork, when it has been attracted and repelled by the one, will not be attracted, but equally repelled by the other. But if the phials were charged, the one through the hook, and the other * through the coating, the ball, when it is repelled from one hook,

* To charge a bottle commodioufly through the coating, place it on a glafs ftand; form a communication from the prime conductor to the coating, and another from the hook to the wall or floor. When it is charged, remove the latter communication before you take hold of the bottle, otherwife great part of the fire will efcape by it.

will

be as ftrongly attracted by the other, and play vigoroufly between them, till both phials are nearly difcharged.

8. When we ufe the terms of *charging* and *difcharging* the phial, it is in compliance with cuftom, and for want of others more fuitable. Since we are of opinion that there is really no more electrical fire in the phial after what is called its *charging*, than before, nor lefs after its *difcharging*; excepting only the fmall fpark that might be given to, and taken from the non-electric matter, if feparated from the bottle, which fpark may not be equal to a five hundredth part of what is called the explofion.

For if, on the explofion, the electrical fire came out of the bottle by one part, and did not enter in again by another, then, if a man, ftanding on wax, and holding the bottle in one hand, takes the fpark by touching the wire hook with the other, the bottle being thereby *difcharged*, the man would be *charged* ; or whatever fire was loft by one, would be found in the other, fince there was no way for its efcape : But the contrary is true.

9. Befides, the phial will not fuffer what is called a *charging*, unlefs as much fire can go out of it one way, as is thrown in by another. A phial cannot be charged ftanding on wax or glafs, or hanging on the prime conductor, unlefs a communication be formed between its coating and the floor.

10. But fufpend two or more phials on the prime conductor, one hanging to the tail of the other ; and a wire from the laft to the floor, an equal number of turns of the

wheel

wheel fhall charge them all equally, and every one as much as one alone would have been. What is driven out at the tail of the firft, ferving to charge the fecond ; what is driven out of the fecond charging the third ; and fo on. By this means a great number of bottles might be charged with the fame labour, and equally high, with one alone, were it not that every bottle receives new fire, and lofes its old with fome reluctance, or rather gives fome fmall re-fiftance to the charging, which in a number of botttles becomes more equal to the charging power, and fo repels the fire back again on the globe, fooner than a fingle bottle would do.

11. When a bottle is charged in the common way, its *infide* and *outfide* furfaces ftand ready, the one to give fire by the hook, the other to receive it by the coating ; the one is full, and ready to throw out, the other empty and extremely hungry ; yet as the firft will not *give out*, unlefs the other can at the fame inftant *receive in* ; fo neither will the latter receive in, unlefs the firft can at the fame inftant give out. When both can be done at once, it is done with inconceivable quicknefs and violence.

12. So a ftrait fpring (though the comparifon does not agree in every particular) when forcibly bent, muft, to re-ftore itfelf, contract that fide which in the bending was extended, and extend that which was contracted ; if either of thefe two operations be hindered, the other cannot be done. But the fpring is not faid to be *charg'd* with elafti-

E   city

city when bent, and difcharged when unbent ; its 'quantity
of elafticity is always the fame.

13. Glafs, in like manner, has, within its fubftance,
always the fame quantity of electrical fire, and that a very
great quantity in proportion to the mafs of glafs, as fhall
be fhewn hereafter.

14. This quantity, proportioned to the glafs, it ftrongly
and obftinately retains, and will have neither more nor lefs
though it will fuffer a change to be made in its parts and
fituation ; *i. e.* we may take away part of it from one
of the fides, provided we throw an equal quantity into the
other.

15. Yet when the fituation of the electrical fire is thus
altered in the glafs ; when fome has been taken from one
fide, and fome added to the other, it will not be at reft or
in its natural ftate, till it is reftored to its original equality.—
And this reftitution cannot be made through the fubftance
of the glafs, but muft be done by a non-electric communication formed without, from furface to furface.

16. Thus, the whole force of the bottle, and power of
giving a fhock, is in the GLASS ITSELF ; the non-electrics
in contact with the two furfaces, ferving only to *give* and
receive to and from the feveral parts of the glafs ; that is, to
give on one fide, and take away from the other.

17. This was difcovered here in the following manner :
Purpofing to analyfe the electrified bottle, in order to find
wherein its ftrength lay, we placed it on glafs, and drew
out the cork and wire which for that purpofe had been

loofe-

loosely put in.   Then taking the bottle in one hand, and
bringing a finger of the other near its mouth, a strong spark
came from the water, and the shock was as violent as if the
wire had remained in it, which shewed that the force did
not lie in the wire.   Then to find if it resided in the water,
being crouded into and condensed in it, as confin'd by the
glass, which had been our former opinion, we electrified
the bottle again, and placing it on glass, drew out the wire
and cork as before ;   then taking up the bottle, we decanted
all its water into an empty bottle, which likewise stood on
glass;   and taking up that other bottle, we expected, if the
force resided in the water, to find a shock from it ;   but
there was none.   We judged then that it must either be
lost in decanting, or remain in the first bottle.   The latter
we found to be true ;   for that bottle on trial gave the shock,
though filled up as it stood with fresh unelectrified water
from a tea-pot.—To find, then, whether glass had this
property merely as glass, or whether the form contributed
any thing to it ;   we took a pane of sash-glass, and laying
it on the hand, placed a plate of lead on its upper surface ;
then electrified that plate, and bringing a finger to it, there
was a spark and shock.   We then took two plates of lead
of equal dimensions, but less than the glass by two inches
every way, and electrified the glass between them, by
electrifying the uppermost lead ;   then separated the glass
from the lead, in doing which, what little fire might
be in the lead was taken out, and the glass being touched
in the electrified parts with a finger, afforded only very

E 2   small.

fmall pricking fparks, but a great number of them might be taken from different places. Then dexteroufly placing it again between the leaden plates, and compleating a circle between the two furfaces, a violent fhock en-fued.——Which demonftrated the power to refide in glafs as glafs, and that the non-electrics in contact ferved only, like the armature of a loadftone, to unite the force of the feveral parts, and bring them at once to any point defired : it being the property of a non-electric, that the whole body inftantly receives or gives what electrical fire is given to or taken from any one of its parts.

18. Upon this we made what we called an *electrical-battery,* confifting of eleven panes of large fafh-glafs, arm'd with thin leaden plates, pafted on each fide, placed verti-cally, and fupported at two inches diftance on filk cords, with thick hooks of leaden wire, one from each fide, ftanding upright, diftant from each other, and convenient communications of wire and chain, from the giving fide of one pane, to the receiving fide of the other ; that fo the whole might be charged together, and with the fame la-bour as one fingle pane ; and another contrivance to bring the giving fides, after charging, in contact with one long wire, and the receivers with another, which two long wires would give the force of all the plates of glafs at once through the body of any animal forming the circle with them. The plates may alfo be difcharged feparately, or any number together that is required. But this machine is not much ufed, as not perfectly anfwering our intention
with

with regard to the eafe of charging, for the reafon given, *Sec.* 10. We made alfo of large glafs panes, magical pictures, and felf-moving animated wheels, prefently to be defcribed.

19. I perceive by the ingenious Mr *Watfon*'s laft book, lately received, that Dr *Bevis* had ufed, before we had, panes of glafs to give a fhock *; though, till that book came to hand, I thought to have communicated it to you as a novelty. The excufe for mentioning it here is, that we tried the experiment differently, drew different confequences from it (for Mr *Watfon* ftill feems to think the fire *accumulated on the non-electric* that is in contact with the glafs, page 72) and, as far as we hitherto know, have carried it farther.

20. The magical picture † is made thus. Having a large metzotinto with a frame and glafs, fuppofe of the KING, (God preferve him) take out the print, and cut a pannel out of it, near two inches diftant from the frame all round. If the cut is through the picture it is not the worfe. With thin pafte, or gum-water, fix the border that is cut off on the infide the glafs, prefling it fmooth and clofe ; then fill up the vacancy by gilding the glafs well with leaf gold, or brafs. Gild likewife the inner edge of the back of the frame all round, except the top part, and form a communication between that gilding and the gilding behind

---

* I have fince heard that Mr *Smeaton* was the firft who made ufe of panes of glafs for that purpofe.

† Contrived by Mr *Kinnerfley*.

the

the glafs : then put in the board, and that fide is finifhed. Turn up the glafs, and gild the fore fide exactly over the back gilding, and when it is dry, cover it, by pafting on the pannel of the picture that hath been cut out, obferving to bring the correfpondent parts of the border and picture together, by which the picture will appear of a piece, as at firft, only part is behind the glafs, and part before.——Hold the picture horizontally by the top, and place a little moveable gilt crown on the king's head. If now the picture be moderately electrified, and another perfon take hold of the frame with one hand, fo that his fingers touch its infide gilding, and with the other hand endeavour to take off the crown, he will receive a terrible blow, and fail in the attempt. If the picture were highly charged, the confequence might perhaps be as fatal * as that of high treafon, for when the fpark is taken through a quire of paper laid on the picture, by means of a wire communication, it makes a fair hole through every fheet, that is, through forty-eight leaves, (though a quire of paper is thought good armour againft the pufh of a fword, or even againft a piftol bullet, and the crack is exceeding loud. The operator, who holds the picture by the upper end, where the infide of the frame is not gilt, to prevent its falling, feels nothing of the fhock, and may touch the face of the picture without danger, which he pretends is a teft of his loyalty.——If a

* We have fince found it fatal to fmall animals, though not to large ones. The biggeft we have yet killed is a hen. 1750.

ring

ring of perſons take the ſhock among them, the experiment is called, *The Conſpirators.*

21. On the principle, in *Sec.* 7, that hooks of bottles, differently charged, will attract and repel differently, is made an electrical wheel, that turns with conſiderable ſtrength. A ſmall upright ſhaft of wood paſſes at right angles through a thin round board, of about twelve inches diameter, and turns on a ſharp point of iron, fixed in the lower end, while a ſtrong wire in the upper end, paſſing through a ſmall hole in a thin braſs plate, keeps the ſhaft truly vertical. About thirty *radii* of equal length, made of ſaſh-glaſs, cut in narrow ſtrips, iſſue horizontally from the circumference of the board, the ends moſt diſtant from the center being about four inches apart.   On the end of every one, a braſs thimble is fixed.   If now the wire of a bottle electrified in the common way, be brought near the circumference of this wheel, it will attract the neareſt thimble, and ſo put the wheel in motion ; that thimble, in paſſing by, receives a ſpark, and thereby being electrified is repelled, and ſo driven forwards ; while a ſecond being attracted, approaches the wire, receives a ſpark, and is driven after the firſt, and ſo on till the wheel has gone once round, when the thimbles before electrified approaching the wire, inſtead of being attracted as they were at firſt, are repelled, and the motion preſently ceaſes.—But if another bottle, which had been charged through the coating, be placed near the ſame wheel, its wire will attract the thimble repelled by the firſt, and thereby double the force that carries the wheel
round ;

round ; and not only taking out the fire that had been communicated to the thimbles by the firſt bottle, but even robbing them of their natural quantity, inſtead of being repelled when they come again towards the firſt bottle, they are more ſtrongly attracted, ſo that the wheel mends its pace, till it goes with great rapidity twelve or fifteen rounds in a minute, and with ſuch ſtrength, as that the weight of one hundred *Spaniſh* dollars with which we once loaded it, did not ſeem in the leaſt to retard its motion.—This is called an electrical jack ; and if a large fowl were ſpitted on the upright ſhaft, it would be carried round before a fire with a motion fit for roaſting.

22. But this wheel, like thoſe driven by wind, water, or weights, moves by a foreign force, to wit, that of the bottles. The ſelf-moving wheel, though conſtructed on the ſame principles, appears more ſurpriſing. 'Tis made of a thin round plate of window-glaſs, ſeventeen inches diameter, well gilt on both ſides, all but two inches next the edge. Two ſmall hemiſpheres of wood are then fixed with cement to the middle of the upper and under ſides, centrally oppoſite, and in each of them a thick ſtrong wire eight or ten inches long, which together make the axis of the wheel. It turns horizontally on a point at the lower end of its axis, which reſts on a bit of braſs cemented within a glaſs ſalt-cellar. The upper end of its axis paſſes through a hole in a thin braſs plate cemented to a long ſtrong piece of glaſs, which keeps it ſix or eight inches diſtant from any non-electric, and has a ſmall ball of wax or metal

metal on its top to keep in the fire. In a circle on the table which ſupports the wheel, are fixed twelve ſmall pillars of glaſs, at about four inches diſtance, with a thimble on the top of each. On the edge of the wheel is a ſmall leaden bullet, communicating by a wire with the gilding of the *upper* ſurface of the wheel ; and about ſix inches from it is another bullet communicating in like manner with the *under* ſurface. When the wheel is to be charged by the upper ſurface, a communication muſt be made from the under ſurface to the table. When it is well charged it begins to move ; the bullet neareſt to a pillar moves towards the thimble on that pillar, and paſſing by, electrifies it, and then puſhes itſelf from it; the ſucceeding bullet, which communicates with the other ſurface of the glaſs, more ſtrongly attracts that thimble, on account of its being before electrified by the other bullet ; and thus the wheel encreaſes its motion till it comes to ſuch a height as that the reſiſtance of the air regulates it. It will go half an hour, and make one minute with another twenty turns in a minute, which is ſix hundred turns in the whole ; the bullet of the upper ſurface giving in each turn twelve ſparks, to the thimbles, which makes ſeven thouſand two hundred ſparks ; and the bullet of the under ſurface receiving as many from the thimbles ; thoſe bullets moving in the time near two thouſand five hundred feet.—The thimbles are well fixed, and in ſo exact a circle, that the bullets may paſs within a very ſmall diſtance of each of them.—If inſtead of two bullets you put eight, four com-

F muni-

municating with the upper furface, and four with the under furface, placed alternately ; which eight, at about fix
inches diftance, completes the circumference, the force and
fwiftnefs will be greatly increafed, the wheel making fifty
turns in a minute ; but then it will not continue moving
fo long.——Thefe wheels may be applied, perhaps, to the
ringing of chimes *, and moving of light-made orreries.

23. A fmall wire bent circularly, with a loop at each
end ; let one end reft againft the under furface of the
wheel, and bring the other end near the upper furface,
it will give a terrible crack, and the force will be difcharged.

24. Every fpark in that manner drawn from the furface
of the wheel, makes a round hole in the gilding, tearing
off a part of it in coming out ; which fhews that the fire
is not accumulated on the gilding, but is in the glafs
itfelf.

25. The gilding being varnifhed over with turpentine
varnifh, the varnifh, though dry and hard, is burnt by the
fpark drawn through it, and gives a ftrong fmell and vifible
fmoke. And when the fpark is drawn through paper, all
round the hole made by it, the paper will be blacked by
the fmoke, which fometimes penetrates feveral of the leaves.
Part of the gilding torn off, is alfo found forcibly driven
into the hole made in the paper by the ftroke.

* This was afterwards done with fuccefs by Mr *Kinnerfley*.

26. It

26. It is amazing to obferve in how fmall a portion of glafs a great electrical force may lie. A thin glafs bubble about an inch diameter, weighing only fix grains, being half filled with water, partly gilt on the outfide, and fur-nifh'd with a wire hook, gives, when electrified, as great a fhock as a man can well bear. As the glafs is thickeft near the orifice, I fuppofe the lower half, which being gilt was electrified and gave the fhock, did not exceed two grains ; for it appeared, when broke, much thinner than the upper half.—If one of thefe thin bottles be electrified by the coating, and the fpark taken out through the gilding, it will break the glafs inwards, at the fame time that it breaks the gilding outwards.

27. And allowing (for the reafons before given, §. 8, 9, 10.) that there is no more electrical fire in a bottle after charging, than before, how great muft be the quantity in this fmall portion of glafs ! It feems as if it were of its very fubftance and effence. Perhaps if that due quantity of electrical fire fo obftinately retained by glafs, could be feparated from it, it would no longer be glafs; it might lofe its tranfparency, or its brittlenefs, or its elafticity.— Experiments may poffibly be invented hereafter, to dif-cover this.

27. We were furprifed at the account given in Mr *Wat-fon*'s book, of a fhock communicated through a great fpace of dry ground, and fufpect there muft be fome metalline quality in the gravel of that ground ; having found that

F 2   fimple

simple dry earth, rammed in a glafs tube, open at both ends, and a wire hook inferted in the earth at each end, the earth and wires making part of a circle, would not conduct the leaft perceptible fhock, and indeed when one wire was electrified, the other hardly fhowed any figns of its being in connection with it *. Even a thoroughly wet pack-thread fometimes fails of conducting a fhock, though it otherwife conducts Electricity very well. A dry cake of ice, or an icicle held between two in a circle, likewife prevents the fhock, which one would not expect, as water conducts it fo perfectly well.—Gilding on a new book, though at firft it conducts the fhock extremely well, yet fails after ten or a dozen experiments, though it appears otherwife in all refpects the fame, which we cannot account for †.

28. There is one experiment more which furprizes us, and is not hitherto fatisfactorily accounted for ; it is this : Place an iron fhot on a glafs ftand, and let a ball of damp cork, fufpended by a filk thread, hang in contact with the fhot. Take a bottle in each hand, one that is electrified through the hook, the other through the coating : Apply the giving wire to the fhot, which will electrify it *pofitive-*

---

* Probably the ground is never fo dry.

† We afterwards found that it failed after one ftroke with a large bottle ; and the continuity of the gold appearing broken, and many of its parts diffipated, the Electricity could not pafs the remaining parts without leaping from part to part through the air, which always refifts the motion of this fluid, and was probably the caufe of the gold's not conducting fo well as before.

ly,

ly, and the cork fhall be repelled : then apply the requiring wire, which will take out the fpark given by the other ; when the cork will return to the fhot : Apply the fame again, and take out another fpark, fo will the fhot be electrified *negatively,* and the cork in that cafe fhall be repelled equally as before. Then apply the giving wire to the fhot, and give the fpark it wanted, fo will the cork return : Give it another, which will be an addition to its natural quantity, fo will the cork be repelled again : And fo may the experiment be repeated as long as there is any charge in the bottles. Which fhews that bodies having lefs than the common quantity of Electricity, repel each other, as well as thofe that have more.

Chagrined a little that we have been hitherto able to produce nothing in this way of ufe to mankind ; and the hot weather coming on, when electrical experiments are not fo agreeable, it is propofed to put an end to them for this feafon, fomewhat humoroufly, in a party of pleafure, on the banks of *Skuylkil* *. Spirits, at the fame time, are to be fired by a fpark fent from fide to fide through the river, without any other conductor than the water ; an experiment which we fome time fince performed, to the amazement of many †. A turkey is to be killed for our

dinner

* The river that wafhes one fide of *Philadelphia,* as the *Delaware* does the other ; both are ornamented with the fummer habitations of the citizens, and the agreeable manfions of the principal people of this colony.

† As the poffibility of this experiment has not been eafily conceived, I

fhall

dinner by the *electrical fhock*, and roafted by the *electrical jack*, before a fire kindled by the *electrified bottle* : when the healths of all the famous electricians in *England, Holland, France*, and *Germany*, are to be drank in * *electrified bumpers*, under the difcharge of guns from the *electrical battery*.

fhall here defcribe it.—Two iron rods, about three feet long, were planted juft within the margin of the river, on the oppofite fides. A thick piece of wire, with a fmall round knob at its end, was fixed to the top of one of the rods, bending downwards, fo as to deliver commodioufly the fpark upon the furface of the fpirit. A fmall wire faftened by one end to the handle of the fpoon, containing the fpirit, was carried a-crofs the river, and fupported in the air by the rope commonly ufed to hold by, in drawing the ferry-boats o-ver. The other end of this wire was tied round the coating of the bottle ; which being charged, the fpark was delivered from the hook to the top of the rod ftanding in the water on that fide. At the fame inftant the rod on the other fide delivered a fpark into the fpoon, and fired the fpirit. The electric fire returning to the coating of the bottle, through the handle of the fpoon and the fupported wire connected with them.

That the electric fire thus actually paffes through the water, has fince been fatisfactorily demonftrated to many by an experiment of Mr *Kinner-fley*'s, performed in a trough of water about ten feet long. The hand being placed under water in the direction of the fpark (which always takes the ftrait or fhorteft courfe) is ftruck and penetrated by it as it paffes.

* An *electrified bumper* is a fmall thin glafs tumbler, near filled with wine, and electrified as the bottle. This when brought to the lips gives a fhock, if the party be clofe fhaved, and does not breathe on the liquor.

April 29,
1749.

LET

L E T T E R XI.

F R O M

Benj. Franklin, *Esq*; of *Philadelphia*.

Oct. 19, 1752.

AS frequent mention is made in public papers from *Europe* of the fuccefs of the *Philadelphia* experiment for drawing the electric fire from clouds by means of pointed rods of iron erected on high buildings, &c. it may be agreeable to the curious to be informed that the fame experiment has fucceeded in *Philadelphia*, though made in a different and more eafy manner, which is as follows :

Make a fmall crofs of two light ftrips of cedar, the arms fo long as to reach to the four corners of a large thin filk handkerchief when extended ; tie the corners of the handkerchief to the extremities of the crofs, fo you have the body of a kite ; which being properly accommodated with a tail, loop, and ftring, will rife in the air, like thofe made of paper ; but this being of filk, is fitter to bear the wet and wind of a thunder-guft without tearing. To the top of the upright ftick of the crofs is to be fixed a very fharp pointed wire, rifing a foot or more

above

above the wood. To the end of the twine, next the hand, is to be tied a filk ribbon, and where the filk and twine join, a key may be faftened. This kite is to be raifed when a thunder guft appears to be coming on, and the perfon who holds the ftring muft ftand within a door or window, or under fome cover, fo that the filk ribbon may not be wet ; and care muft be taken that the twine does not touch the frame of the door or window. As foon as any of the thunder clouds come over the kite, the pointed wire will draw the electric fire from them, and the kite, with all the twine, will be electrified, and the loofe filaments of the twine will ftand out every way, and be attracted by an approaching finger. And when the rain has wet the kite and twine, fo that it can conduct the electric fire freely, you will find it ftream out plentifully from the key on the approach of your knuckle. At this key the phial may be charged ; and from electric fire thus obtained, fpirits may be kindled, and all the other electric experiments be performed, which are ufually done by the help of a rubbed glafs globe or tube, and thereby the fame-nefs of the electric matter with that of lightening com-pletely demonftrated.

B. F.

L E T-

JOSEPH HENRY

1797-1878

Well into the nineteenth century American science existed, where it existed at all, either as a genteel pastime or as an adjunct to the urgent needs of the new nation—agriculture, navigation, exploration. The best research was usually done in fields serving these practical interests, and the closest approach to physics was work in positional astronomy, meteorology, geology and the like. Joseph Henry arose from this tradition and quickly surpassed it.

Henry's parents both came to America from Scotland as children in the turbulent year 1775. His father, a poor laborer, died when the son was still a boy, and young Henry was soon apprenticed out to a watchmaker and silversmith in Albany, New York. Nothing distinguished Henry from other half-educated young craftsmen except strong interests in amateur theater and in reading. But at the age of sixteen he chanced to read a book of *Popular Lectures on Experimental Philosophy, Astronomy, and Chemistry*. Fascinated by this glimpse of science, he resolved to learn more.

In 1819 he enrolled in the Albany Academy. In modern terms this would be closest to a private secondary school, but in early American terms it offered the equivalent of a college education. Henry went beyond the coursework, avidly reading books in every area of science and many other fields. He meanwhile made use of each increment in his learning to support himself, progressing from country schoolmaster through tutor of wealthy youths and road surveyor to Professor of Mathematics and Natural Philosophy at the Albany Academy.

A few years later he described his situation in a letter: ". . . My duties at the Academy are not well suited to my taste. I am engaged on an average seven hours in a day, one half of the time in teaching the higher classes in Mathematics, and the other half in the drudgery of instructing a class of sixty boys in the elements of Arithmetic." Nevertheless he found a little time, a little space, and a little money to do research.

Like most scientists of his day Henry was no specialist, and matters like meteorology took his attention throughout his life. At the Albany Academy he prospected in various areas of physical science and almost at once struck his vein of gold: electromagnetism. He was inspired in part by reports of a rudimentary electromagnet constructed in Europe and in part by theoretical ideas based on his reading of Ampère. He began to build electromagnets which, for the first time, were wound with many strands and layers of insulated wire. (According to legend, for insulation he used silk strips torn from his wife's petticoats.) He carefully distinguished between "quantity" circuits of high amperage and "intensity" circuits of high voltage; he worked out what we now call impedance matching; he independently found a preliminary sort of Ohm's law. Understanding electrical circuits better than any of his predecessors, he built an electromagnet that could hold up to 750 pounds of iron, yet required a battery of only modest size and cost.

Electromagnets of such efficiency were a marvelous new tool for science. Henry used them to build "philosophical toys" which foreshadowed the telegraph and the electric motor. The strong magnetic fields were equally valuable for fundamental research and allowed him to discover mutual induction and self-induction. All this soon brought Henry international fame. His reputation would have been still greater had it not been for Faraday, who, with equal genius and better working conditions in England, had anticipated some of Henry's discoveries.

In 1832 Henry went to Princeton (then called the College of New Jersey) as professor of natural philosophy, one of the handful of positions in America which would give a physicist enough time for research. Here he did much solid work on electricity and magnetism and also published papers on capillarity, phosphorescence, the heat of sunspots, the aurora, and more. He was widely respected, usually a reticent man but outspoken when the needs of science were at stake. Throughout his life he held devoutly to the Presbyterianism in which he was raised. Over the years he attracted a number of close friends; he worked with them to raise the level of pure science in America, which they considered dismally low.

In 1846 he accepted the post of Secretary in the new and unformed Smithsonian Institution. Much of his life thereafter was spent in giving governmental bodies scientific advice, particularly on practical matters, and in working to keep the Smithsonian from becoming a purely curatorial institution. As director of the Smithsonian and as President of the fledgling National Academy of Sciences from 1867 to his death, Henry worked to ensure that America would support science — not only applied but also pure science, not only amateur but also rigorous and professional science.

The following excerpt is from the *American Journal of Science* (vol. 22, 1832, p. 403-08), published by Benjamin Silliman of Yale, a magazine which for many decades was the leading American scientific journal. The second selection is part of a longer work presented to the American Philosophical Society and published in its *Transactions* (n.s. vol. 6, 1839, p. 303-37); it shows Henry masterfully dealing with the problem of induction and electrical currents, using no detecting instrument more sensitive than the human body.

THE

AMERICAN JOURNAL

OF

SCIENCE AND ARTS.

CONDUCTED BY

BENJAMIN SILLIMAN, M. D. LL. D.

Prof. Chem., Min., &c. in Yale Coll.; Cor. Mem. Soc. Arts, Man. and Com; and
For. Mem. Geol. Soc., London; Mem. Roy. Min. Soc., Dresden; Nat. Hist.
Soc., Halle; Imp. Agric. Soc., Moscow; Hon. Mem. Lin. Soc., Paris;
Nat. Hist. Soc. Belfast, Ire.; Phil. and Lit. Soc. Bristol, Eng.;
Mem. of various Lit. and Scien. Soc. in America.

VOL. XXII.—JULY, 1832.

NEW HAVEN:

Published and Sold by HEZEKIAH HOWE & Co. and A. H. MALTBY.
Baltimore, E. J. COALE & J. S. LITTELL.—Philadelphia, E. LITTELL and
CAREY & HART.—New York, G. & C. & H. CARVILL—Boston, HIL-
LIARD, GRAY, LITTLE & WILKINS.

PRINTED BY HEZEKIAH HOWE & CO.

APPENDIX.

On the Production of Currents and Sparks of Electricity from Magnetism; by Prof. J. HENRY.

ALTHOUGH the discoveries of Oersted, Arago, Faraday, and others, have placed the intimate connection of electricity and magnetism in a most striking point of view, and although the theory of Ampere has referred all the phenomena of both these departments of science to the same general laws, yet until lately one thing remained to be proved by experiment, in order more fully to establish their identity; namely, the possibility of producing electrical effects from magnetism. It is well known that surprising magnetic results can readily be obtained from electricity, and at first sight it might be supposed that electrical effects could with equal facility be produced from magnetism; but such has not been found to be the case, for although the experiment has often been attempted, it has nearly as often failed.

It early occurred to me, that if galvanic magnets, on my plan, were substituted for ordinary magnets, in researches of this kind, more success might be expected. Besides their great power, these magnets possess other properties, which render them important instruments in the hands of the experimenter; their polarity can be instantaneously reversed, and their magnetism suddenly destroyed or called into full action, according as the occasion may require. With this view, I commenced, last August, the construction of a much larger galvanic magnet than, to my knowledge, had before been attempted, and also made preparations for a series of experiments with it on a large scale, in reference to the production of electricity from magnetism. I was, however, at that time, accidentally interrupted in the prosecution of these experiments, and have not been able since to resume them, until within the last few weeks, and then on a much smaller scale than was at first intended. In the mean time, it has been announced in the 117th number of the Library of Useful Knowledge, that the result so much sought after has at length been found by Mr. Faraday of the Royal Institution. It states that he has established the general fact, that when a piece of metal is moved in any direction, in front of a magnetic pole, electrical currents are developed in the metal, which pass in a direction at right angles to its own motion, and also that the application of this principle affords a complete and satisfactory explanation of the phenomena of magnetic rotation. No detail is given of the experiments, and it is somewhat surprising that results so interesting, and which certainly form a new era in the history of electricity and magnetism, should not have been more fully described before this time in some of the English publications; the only mention I have found of them is the following short account from the Annals of Philosophy for April, under the head of Proceedings of the Royal Institution.

" Feb. 17.—Mr. Faraday gave an account of the first two parts of his researches in electricity; namely, Volta-electric induction and magneto-electric induction. If two wires, A and B, be placed side by side, but not in contact, and a Voltaic current be passed through A, there is instantly a current produced by induction in B, in the opposite direction. Although the principal current in A be continued, still the secondary current in B is not found to accompany it, for it ceases after the first moment, but when the principal current is stopped then there is a second current produced in B, in the opposite direction to that of the first produced by the inductive action, or in the same direction as that of the principal current.

" If a wire, connected at both extremities with a galvanometer, be coiled in the form of a helix around a magnet, no current of electricity takes place in it. This is an experiment which has been made by various persons hundreds of times, in the hope of evolving electricity from magnetism, and as in other cases in which the wishes of the experimenter and the facts are opposed to each other, has given rise to very conflicting conclusions. But if the magnet be withdrawn from or introduced into such a helix, a current of electricity is produced *whilst the magnet is in motion*, and is rendered evident by the deflection of the galvanometer. If a single wire be passed by a magnetic pole, a current of electricity is induced through it which can be rendered sensible."*

Before having any knowledge of the method given in the above account, I had succeeded in producing electrical effects in the following manner, which differs from that employed by Mr. Faraday, and which appears to me to develope some new and interesting facts. A piece of copper wire, about thirty feet long and covered with elastic varnish, was closely coiled around the middle of the soft iron armature of the galvanic magnet, described in Vol. XIX of the American Journal of Science, and which, when excited, will readily

---

* This extract will also be found on page 386 of this Journal.—*Ed.*

sustain between six hundred and seven hundred pounds. The wire was wound upon itself so as to occupy only about one inch of the length of the armature which is seven inches in all. The armature, thus furnished with the wire, was placed in its proper position across the ends of the galvanic magnet, and there fastened so that no motion could take place. The two projecting ends of the helix were dipped into two cups of mercury, and there connected with a distant galvanometer by means of two copper wires, each about forty feet long. This arrangement being completed, I stationed myself near the galvanometer and directed an assistant at a given word to immerse suddenly, in a vessel of dilute acid, the galvanic battery attached to the magnet. At the instant of immersion, the north end of the needle was deflected 30° to the west, indicating a current of electricity from the helix surrounding the armature. The effect, however, appeared only as a single impulse, for the needle, after a few oscillations, resumed its former undisturbed position in the magnetic meridian, although the galvanic action of the battery, and consequently the magnetic power was still continued. I was, however, much surprised to see the needle suddenly deflected from a state of rest to about 20° to the east, or in a contrary direction when the battery was withdrawn from the acid, and again deflected to the west when it was re-immersed. This operation was repeated many times in succession, and uniformly with the same result, the armature, the whole time, remaining immoveably attached to the poles of the magnet, no motion being required to produce the effect, as it appeared to take place only in consequence of the instantaneous development of the magnetic action in one, and the sudden cessation of it in the other.

This experiment illustrates most strikingly the reciprocal action of the two principles of electricity and magnetism, if indeed it does not establish their absolute identity. In the first place, magnetism is developed in the soft iron of the galvanic magnet by the action of the currents of electricity from the battery, and secondly the armature, rendered magnetic by contact with the poles of the magnet, induces in its turn, currents of electricity in the helix which surrounds it; we have thus as it were electricity converted into magnetism and this magnetism again into electricity.

Another fact was observed which is somewhat interesting in as much as it serves, in some respects, to generalize the phenomena. After the battery had been withdrawn from the acid, and the needle of the galvanometer suffered to come to a state of rest after the resulting deflection, it was again deflected in the same direction by partially detaching the armature from the poles of the magnet to which it continued to adhere from the action of the residual magnetism, and in this way, a series of deflections, all in the same direction, was produced by merely slipping off the armature, by degrees, until the contact was entirely broken. The following extract from the register of the experiments exhibits the relative deflections observed in one experiment of this kind.

At the instant of immersion of the battery, deflec. 40° west.

"   "   "   "   "   "   18   east.

Armature partially detached,   "   7   east.

Armature entirely detached,   "   12   east.

The effect was reversed in another experiment, in which the needle was turned to the west in a series of deflections by dipping the battery but a small distance into the acid at first and afterwards immersing it by degrees.

From the foregoing facts, it appears that a current of electricity is produced, for an instant, in a helix of copper wire surrounding a piece of soft iron whenever magnetism is induced in the iron; and a current in an opposite direction when the magnetic action ceases; also that an instantaneous current in one or the other direction accompanies every change in the magnetic intensity of the iron.

Since reading the account before given of Mr. Faraday's method of producing electrical currents I have attempted to combine the effects of motion and induction; for this purpose a rod of soft iron ten inches long and one inch and a quarter in diameter, was attached to a common turning lathe, and surrounded with four helices of copper wire in such a manner that it could be suddenly and powerfully magnetized, while in rapid motion, by transmitting galvanic currents through three of the helices; the fourth being connected with the distant galvanometer was intended to transmit the current of induced electricity : all the helices were stationary while the iron rod revolved on its axis within them. From a number of trials in succession, first with the rod in one direction then in the opposite, and next in a state of rest, it was concluded that no perceptible effect was produced on the intensity of the *magneto-electric* current by a rotatory motion of the iron combined with its sudden magnetization.

The same apparatus however furnished the means of measuring separately the relative power of motion and induction in producing electrical currents. The iron rod was first magnetized by currents

43

JOSEPH HENRY

through the helices attached to the battery and while in this state one of its ends was quickly introduced into the helix connected with the galvanometer; the deflection of the needle, in this case, was seven degrees. The end of the rod was next introduced into the same helix while in its natural state and then suddenly magnetized; the deflection, in this instance amounted to thirty degrees, shewing a great superiority in the method of induction.

The next attempt was to increase the *magneto-electric* effect while the magnetic power remained the same, and in this I was more successful. Two iron rods six inches long and one inch in diameter, were each surrounded by two helices and then placed perpendicularly on the face of the armature, and between it and the poles of the magnet so that each rod formed as it were a prolongation of the poles, and to these the armature adhered when the magnet was excited. With this arrangement, a current from one helix produced a deflection of thirty seven degrees; from two helices both on the same rod fifty two degrees, and from three fifty nine degrees: but when four helices were used, the deflection was only fifty five degrees, and when to these were added the helix of smaller wire around the armature, the deflection was no more than thirty degrees. This result may perhaps have been somewhat affected by the want of proper insulation in the several spires of the helices, it however establishes the fact that an increase in the electric current is produced by using at least two or three helices instead of one. The same principle was applied to another arrangement which seems to afford the maximum of electric development from a given magnetic power; in place of the two pieces of iron and the armature used in the last experiments, the poles of the magnet were connected by a single rod of iron, bent into the form of a horse-shoe, and its extremities filed perfectly flat so as to come in perfect contact with the faces of the poles: around the middle of the arch of this horse-shoe, two strands of copper wire were tightly coiled one over the other. A current from one of these helices deflected the needle one hundred degrees, and when both were used the needle was deflected with such force as to make a complete circuit. But the most surprising effect was produced when instead of passing the current through the long wires to the galvanometer, the opposite ends of the helices were held nearly in contact with each other, and the magnet suddenly excited; in this case a small but vivid spark was seen to pass between the ends of the wires and this effect was repeated as often as the state of intensity of the magnet was changed.

In these experiments the connection of the battery with the wires from the magnet was not formed by soldering, but by two cups of mercury which permitted the galvanic action on the magnet to be instantaneously suspended and the polarity to be changed and rechanged without removing the battery from the acid; a succession of vivid sparks was obtained by rapidly interrupting and forming the communication by means of one of these cups; but the greatest effect was produced when the magnetism was entirely destroyed and instantaneously reproduced by a change of polarity.

It appears from the May No. of the Annals of Philosophy, that I have been anticipated in this experiment of drawing sparks from the magnet by Mr. James D. Forbes of Edinburgh, who obtained a spark* on the 30th of March; my experiments being made during the last two weeks of June. A simple notification of his result is given, without any account of the experiment, which is reserved for a communication to the Royal Society of Edinburgh; my result is therefore entirely independent of his and was undoubtedly obtained by a different process.

I have made several other experiments in relation to the same subject, but which more important duties will not permit me to verify in time for this paper. I may however mention one fact which I have not seen noticed in any work and which appears to me to belong to the same class of phænomena as those before described: it is this; when a small battery is moderately excited by diluted acid and its poles, which must be terminated by cups of mercury, are connected by a copper wire not more than a foot in length, no spark is perceived when the connection is either formed or broken: but if a wire thirty or forty feet long be used, instead of the short wire, though no spark will be perceptible when the connection is made, yet when it is broken by drawing one end of the wire from its cup of mercury a vivid spark is produced. If the action of the battery be very intense, a spark will be given by the short wire; in this case it is only necessary to wait a few minutes until the action partially subsides and until no more sparks are given from the short wire; if the long wire be now substituted a spark will again be obtained. The effect appears somewhat increased by coiling the wire into a helix; it seems also to depend in some measure on the length and thickness of the wire; I can account for these phænomena only by supposing the long wire to become charged with electricity which by its reaction on itself projects a spark when the connection is broken.

---

* From a natural magnet.

45

JOSEPH HENRY

ARTICLE IX.

Contributions to Electricity and Magnetism. By Joseph Henry, Professor of Natural Philosophy in the College of New Jersey, Princeton.

No. III.—On Electro-Dynamic Induction. Read November 2, 1838.

INTRODUCTION.

1. SINCE my investigations in reference to the influence of a spiral conductor, in increasing the intensity of a galvanic current, were submitted to the Society, the valuable paper of Dr Faraday, on the same subject, has been published, and also various modifications of the principle have been made by Sturgeon, Masson, Page and others, to increase the effects. The spiral conductor has likewise been applied by Cav. Antinori to produce a spark by the action of a thermo-electrical pile; and Mr Watkins has succeeded in exhibiting all the phenomena of hydro-electricity by the same means. Although the principle has been much extended by the researches of Dr Faraday, yet I am happy to state that the results obtained by this distinguished philosopher are not at variance with those given in my paper.

2. I now offer to the Society a new series of investigations in the same line, which I hope may also be considered of sufficient importance to merit a place in the Transactions.

3. The primary object of these investigations was to discover, if

VI.—4 A

possible, inductive actions in common electricity analogous to those found in galvanism. For this purpose a series of experiments was commenced in the spring of 1836, but I was at that time diverted, in part, from the immediate object of my research, by a new investigation of the phenomenon known in common electricity by the name of the lateral discharge. Circumstances prevented my doing any thing further, in the way of experiment, until April last, when most of the results which I now offer to the Society were obtained. The investigations are not as complete, in several points, as I could wish, but as my duties will not permit me to resume the subject for some months to come, I therefore present them as they are; knowing, from the interest excited by this branch of science in every part of the world, that the errors which may exist will soon be detected, and the truths be further developed.

4. The experiments are given nearly in the order in which they were made; and in general they are accompanied by the reflections which led to the several steps of the investigation. The whole series is divided, for convenience of arrangement, into six sections, although the subject may be considered as consisting, principally, of two parts. The first relating to a new examination of the induction of galvanic currents; and the second to the discovery of analogous results in the discharge of ordinary electricity.*

5. The principal articles of apparatus used in the experiments, consist of a number of flat coils of copper riband, which will be desig-

Fig. 1.

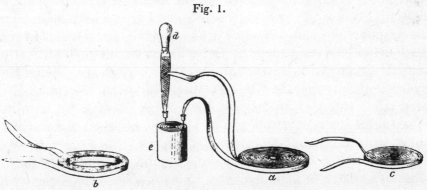

a represents coil No. 1, *b* coil No. 2, and *c* coil No. 3; *e* the battery, *d* the rasp.

---

* The several paragraphs are numbered in succession, from the first to the last, after the mode adopted by Mr Faraday, for convenience of reference.

nated by the names of coil No. 1, coil No. 2, &c.; also of several coils
of long wire; and these, to distinguish them from the ribands, will be
called helix No. 1, helix No. 2, &c.

6. Coil No. 1 is formed of thirteen pounds of copper plate, one inch
and a half wide and ninety-three feet long.   It is well covered with
two coatings of silk, and was generally used in the form represented in
Fig. 1, which is that of a flat spiral sixteen inches in diameter.   It
was however sometimes formed into a ring of larger diameter, as is
shown in Fig. 4, Section III.

7. Coil No. 2 is also formed of copper plate, of the same width and
thickness as coil No. 1.   It is, however, only sixty feet long.   Its
form is shown at *b*, Fig. 1.   The opening at the centre is sufficient to
admit helix No. 1.   Coils No. 3, 4, 5, 6, &c. are all about sixty feet
long, and of copper plate of the same thickness, but of half the width
of coil No. 1.

8. Helix No. 1 consists of sixteen hundred and sixty yards of copper wire, $\frac{1}{45}$th of an inch in diameter.   No. 2, of nine hundred and

Fig. 2.

ninety yards; and No. 3, of three
hundred and fifty yards, of the same
wire.   These helices are shown in
Fig. 2, and are so adjusted in size

a represents helix No. 1, *b* helix No. 2, *c* helix No. 3.

as to fit into each other; thus form-
ing one long helix of three thousand yards: or, by using them separately, and in different combinations, seven helices of different lengths.
The wire is covered with cotton thread, saturated with beeswax, and
between each stratum of spires a coating of silk is interposed.

9. Helix No. 4 is shown at *a*, Fig. 4, Section III.; it is formed of five hundred and forty-six yards of wire, $\frac{1}{45}$th of an inch in diameter, the several
spires of which are insulated by a coating of cement.   Helix No. 5
consists of fifteen hundred yards of silvered copper wire, $\frac{1}{133}$th of an inch
in diameter, covered with cotton, and is of the form of No. 4.

10. Besides these I was favoured with the loan of a large spool of
copper wire, covered with cotton, $\frac{1}{16}$th of an inch in diameter, and five
miles long.   It is wound on a small axis of iron, and forms a solid cylinder of wire, eighteen inches long, and thirteen in diameter.

11. For determining the direction of induced currents, a magnetiz-

ing spiral was generally used, which consists of about thirty spires of copper wire, in the form of a cylinder, and so small as just to admit a sewing needle into the axis.

12. Also a small horseshoe is frequently referred to, which is formed of a piece of soft iron, about three inches long, and $\frac{2}{3}$ths of an inch thick ; each leg is surrounded with about five feet of copper bell wire. This length is so small, that only a current of electricity of considerable quantity can develope the magnetism of the iron. The instrument is used for indicating the existence of such a current.

13. The battery used in most of the experiments is shown in Fig. 1. It is formed of three concentric cylinders of copper, and two interposed cylinders of zinc. It is about eight inches high, five inches in diameter, and exposes about one square foot and three quarters of zinc surface, estimating both sides of the metal. In some of the experiments a larger battery was used, weakly charged, but all the results mentioned in the paper, except those with a Cruickshank trough, can be obtained with one or two batteries of the above size, particularly if excited by a strong solution. The manner of interrupting the circuit of the conductor by means of a rasp, *b*, is shown in the same Figure.

SECTION I.

Conditions which influence the induction of a Current on itself.

14. The phenomenon of the spiral conductor is at present known by the name of the induction of a current on itself, to distinguish it from the induction of the secondary current, discovered by Dr Faraday. The two, however, belong to the same class, and experiments render it probable that the spark given by the long conductor is, from the natural electricity of the metal, disturbed for an instant by the induction of the primary current. Before proceeding to the other parts of these investigations, it is important to state the results of a number of preliminary experiments, made to determine more definitely the conditions which influence the action of the spiral conductor.

15. When the electricity is of low intensity, as in the case of the thermo-electrical pile, or a large single battery weakly excited with dilute acid, the flat riband coil No. 1, ninety-three feet long, is found to

give the most brilliant deflagrations, and the loudest snaps from a sur- face of mercury.   The shocks, with this arrangement, are, however, very feeble, and can only be felt in the fingers or through the tongue.

16. The induced current in a short coil, which thus produces defla- gration, but not shocks, may, for distinction, be called one of quantity.

17. When the length of the coil is increased, the battery continuing the same, the deflagrating power decreases, while the intensity of the shock continually increases.   With five riband coils, making an aggre- gate length of three hundred feet, and the small battery, Fig. 1, the de- flagration is less than with coil No. 1, but the shocks are more in- tense.

18. There is, however, a limit to this increase of intensity of the shock, and this takes place when the increased resistance or diminished conduction of the lengthened coil begins to counteract the influence of the increasing length of the current.   The following experiment illustrates this fact.   A coil of copper wire $\frac{1}{16}$th of an inch in diame- ter, was increased in length by successive additions of about thirty-two feet at a time.   After the first two lengths, or sixty-four feet, the bril- liancy of the spark began to decline, but the shocks constantly in- creased in intensity, until a length of five hundred and seventy-five feet was obtained, when the shocks also began to decline.   This was then the proper length to produce the maximum effect with a single battery, and a wire of the above diameter.

19. When the intensity of the electricity of the battery is increased, the action of the short riband coil decreases.   With a Cruickshank's trough of sixty plates, four inches square, scarcely any peculiar effect can be observed, when the coil forms a part of the circuit.   If how- ever the length of the coil be increased in proportion to the intensity of the current, then the inductive influence becomes apparent.   When the current, from ten plates of the above mentioned trough, was passed through the wire of the large spool (10), the induced shock was too severe to be taken through the body.   Again, when a small trough of twenty-five one-inch plates, which alone would give but a very feeble shock, was used with helix No. 1, an intense shock was received from the induction, when the contact was broken.   Also a slight shock in this arrangement is given when the contact is formed, but it is very feeble

VI.—4 B

in comparison with the other.   The spark, however, with the long wire and compound battery is not as brilliant as with the single battery and the short riband coil.

20. When the shock is produced from a long wire, as in the last experiments, the size of the plates of the battery may be very much reduced, without a corresponding reduction of the intensity of the shock.   This is shown in an experiment with the large spool of wire (10). A very small compound battery was formed of six pieces of copper bell wire, about one inch and a half long, and an equal number of pieces of zinc of the same size.   When the current from this was passed through the five miles of the wire of the spool, the induced shock was given at once to twenty-six persons joining hands.   This astonishing effect placed the action of a coil in a striking point of view.

21. With the same spool and the single battery used in the former experiments, no shock, or at most a very feeble one, could be obtained. A current, however, was found to pass through the whole length, by its action on the galvanometer; but it was not sufficiently powerful to induce a current which could counteract the resistance of so long a wire.

22. The induced current in these experiments may be considered as one of *considerable intensity*, and *small quantity*.

23. The form of the coil has considerable influence on the intensity of the action.   In the experiments of Dr Faraday, a long cylindrical coil of thick copper wire, inclosing a rod of soft iron, was used.   This form produces the greatest effect when magnetic reaction is employed ; but in the case of simple galvanic induction, I have found the form of the coils and helices represented in the figures most effectual.   The several spires are more nearly approximated, and therefore they exert a greater mutual influence.   In some cases, as will be seen hereafter, the ring form, shown in Fig. 4, is most effectual.

24. In all cases the several spires of the coil should be well insulated, for although in magnetizing soft iron, and in analogous experiments, the touching of two spires is not attended with any great reduction of action; yet in the case of the induced current, as will be shown in the progress of these investigations, a single contact of two spires is sometimes sufficient to neutralize the whole effect.

51

JOSEPH HENRY

25. It must be recollected that all the experiments with these coils and helices, unless otherwise mentioned, are made without the reaction of iron temporarily magnetized; since the introduction of this would, in some cases, interfere with the action, and render the results more complex.

SECTION II.

Conditions which influence the production of Secondary Currents.

26. The secondary currents, as it is well known, were discovered in the induction of magnetism and electricity, by Dr Faraday, in 1831. But he was at that time urged to the exploration of new, and apparently richer veins of science, and left this branch to be traced by others.   Since then, however, attention has been almost exclusively directed to one part of the subject, namely, the induction from magnetism, and the perfection of the magneto-electrical machine.   And I know of no attempts, except my own, to review and extend the purely electrical part of Dr Faraday's admirable discovery.

27. The energetic action of the flat coil, in producing the induction of a current on itself, led me to conclude that it would also be the most proper means for the exhibition and study of the phenomena of the secondary galvanic currents.

28. For this purpose coil No. 1 was arranged to receive the current from the small battery, and coil No. 2 placed on this, with a plate of glass interposed to insure perfect insulation; as often as the circuit of No. 1 was interrupted, a powerful secondary current was induced in No. 2.   The arrangement is the same as that exhibited in Fig. 3, with the exception that in this the compound helix is represented as receiving the induction, instead of coil No. 2.

Fig. 3.

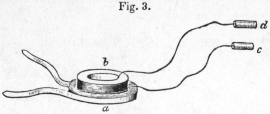

a represents coil No. 1, *b* helix No. 1, and *c, d,* handles for receiving the shock.

29. When the ends of the second coil were rubbed together, a spark was produced at the opening.   When the same ends were joined by

the magnetizing spiral (11), the inclosed needle became strongly magnetic. Also when the secondary current was passed through the wires of the iron horseshoe (12), magnetism was developed; and when the ends of the second coil were attached to a small decomposing apparatus, of the kind which accompanies the magneto-electrical machine, a stream of gas was given off at each pole. The shock, however, from this coil is very feeble, and can scarcely be felt above the fingers.

30. This current has therefore the properties of one of moderate intensity, but considerable quantity.

31. Coil No. 1 remaining as before, a longer coil, formed by uniting Nos. 3, 4 and 5, was substituted for No. 2. With this arrangement, the spark produced when the ends were rubbed together, was not as brilliant as before; the magnetizing power was much less; decomposition was nearly the same, but the shocks were more powerful, or, in other words, the intensity of the induced current was increased by an increase of the length of the coil, while the quantity was apparently decreased.

32. A compound helix, formed by uniting Nos. 1 and 2, and therefore containing two thousand six hundred and fifty yards of wire, was next placed on coil No. 1. The weight of this helix happened to be precisely the same as that of coil No. 2, and hence the different effects of the same quantity of metal in the two forms of a long and short conductor, could be compared. With this arrangement the magnetizing effects, with the apparatus before mentioned, disappeared. The sparks were much smaller, and also the decomposition less, than with the short coil; but the shock was almost too intense to be received with impunity, except through the fingers of one hand. A circuit of fifty-six of the students of the senior class, received it at once from a single rupture of the battery current, as if from the discharge of a Leyden jar weakly charged. The secondary current in this case was one of small quantity, but of great intensity.

33. The following experiment is important in establishing the fact of a limit to the increase of the intensity of the shock, as well as the power of decomposition, with a wire of a given diameter. Helix No. 5, which consists of wire only $\frac{1}{123}$th of an inch in diameter, was placed

on coil No. 2, and its length increased to about seven hundred yards. With this extent of wire, neither decomposition nor magnetism could be obtained, but shocks were given of a peculiarly pungent nature; they did not however produce much muscular action.   The wire of the helix was further increased to about fifteen hundred yards; the shock was now found to be scarcely perceptible, in the fingers.

34. As a counterpart to the last experiment, coil No. 1 was formed into a ring of sufficient internal diameter to admit the great spool of wire (11), and with the whole length of this (which, as has before been stated, is five miles) the shock was found so intense as to be felt at the shoulder, when passed only through the forefinger and thumb. Sparks and decomposition were also produced, and needles rendered magnetic.   The wire of this spool is $\frac{1}{16}$th of an inch thick, and we therefore see from this experiment, that by increasing the diameter of the wire, its length may also be much increased, with an increased effect.

35. The fact (33) that the induced current is diminished by a further increase of the wire, after a certain length has been attained, is important in the construction of the magneto-electrical machine, since the same effect is produced in the induction of magnetism.   Dr Goddard of Philadelphia, to whom I am indebted for coil No. 5, found that when its whole length was wound on the iron of a temporary magnet, no shocks could be obtained.   The wire of the machine may therefore be of such a length, relative to its diameter, as to produce shocks, but no decomposition; and if the length be still further increased, the power of giving shocks may also become neutralized.

36. The inductive action of coil No. 1, in the foregoing experiments, is precisely the same as that of a temporary magnet in the case of the magneto-electrical machine.   A short thick wire around the armature gives brilliant deflagrations, but a long one produces shocks.   This fact, I believe, was first discovered by my friend Mr Saxton, and afterwards investigated by Sturgeon and Lentz.

37. We might, at first sight, conclude, from the perfect similarity of these effects, that the currents which, according to the theory of Ampere, exist in the magnet, are like those in the short coil, of great

VI.—4 c

quantity and feeble intensity; but succeeding experiments will show that this is not necessarily the case.

38. All the experiments given in this section have thus far been made with a battery of a single element. This condition was now changed, and a Cruickshank trough of sixty pairs substituted. When the current from this was passed through the riband coil No. 1, no indication, or a very feeble one, was given of a secondary current in any of the coils or helices, arranged as in the preceding experiments. The length of the coil, in this case, was not commensurate with the intensity of the current from the battery. But when the long helix, No. 1, was placed instead of coil No. 1, a powerful inductive action was produced on each of the articles, as before.

39. First, helices No. 2 and 3 were united into one, and placed within helix No. 1, which still conducted the battery current. With this disposition a secondary current was produced, which gave intense shocks but feeble decomposition, and no magnetism in the soft iron horseshoe. It was therefore one of intensity, and was induced by a battery current also of intensity.

40. Instead of the helix used in the last experiment for receiving the induction, one of the coils (No. 3) was now placed on helix No. 1, the battery remaining as before. With this arrangement the induced current gave no shocks, but it magnetized the small horseshoe; and when the ends of the coil were rubbed together, produced bright sparks. It had therefore the properties of a current of quantity; and it was produced by the induction of a current, from the battery, of intensity.

41. This experiment was considered of so much importance, that it was varied and repeated many times, but always with the same result; it therefore establishes the fact *that an intensity current can induce one of quantity*, and, by the preceding experiments, the converse has also been shown, that *a quantity current can induce one of intensity*.

42. This fact appears to have an important bearing on the law of the inductive action, and would seem to favour the supposition that the lower coil, in the two experiments with the long and short secon-

dary conductors, exerted the same amount of inductive force, and that in one case this was expended (to use the language of theory) in giving a great velocity to a small quantity of the fluid, and in the other in producing a slower motion in a larger current; but in the two cases, were it not for the increased resistance to conduction in the longer wire, the quantity multiplied by the velocity would be the same. This, however, is as yet an hypothesis, but it enables us to conceive how intensity and quantity may both be produced from the same induction.

43. From some of the foregoing experiments we may conclude, that the quantity of electricity in motion in the helix is really less than in the coil, of the same weight of metal; but this may possibly be owing simply to the greater resistance offered by the longer wire. It would also appear, if the above reasoning be correct, that to produce the most energetic physiological effects, only a small quantity of electricity, moving with great velocity, is necessary.

44.   In this and the preceding section, I have attempted to give only the general conditions which influence the galvanic induction. To establish the law would require a great number of more refined experiments, and the consideration of several circumstances which would affect the results, such as the conduction of the wires, the constant state of the battery, the method of breaking the circuit with perfect regularity, and also more perfect means than we now possess of measuring the amount of the inductive action; all these circumstances render the problem very complex.

SECTION III.

On the Induction of Secondary Currents at a distance.

45. In the experiments given in the two preceding Sections. the conductor which received the induction, was separated from that which transmitted the primary current by the thickness only of a pane of glass; but the action from this arrangement was so energetic, that I was naturally led to try the effect at a greater distance.

46. For this purpose coil No. 1 was formed into a ring of about two

Fig. 4.

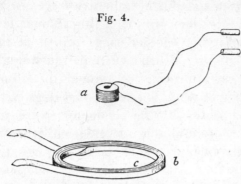

a represents helix No. 4, *b* coil No. 1, in the form of a ring.

feet in diameter, and helix No. 4 placed as is shown in the figure. When the helix was at the distance of about sixteen inches from the middle of the plane of the ring, shocks could be perceived through the tongue, and these rapidly increased in intensity as the helix was lowered, and when it reached the plane of the ring they were quite severe. The effect, however, was still greater, when the helix was moved from the centre to the inner circumference, as at *c*: but when it was placed without the ring, in contact with the outer circumference, at *b*, the shocks were very slight; and when placed within, but its axis at right angles to that of the ring, not the least effect could be observed.

47. With a little reflection, it will be evident that this arrangement is not the most favourable for exhibiting the induction at a distance, since the side of the ring, for example, at *c*, tends to produce a current revolving in one direction in the near side of the helix, and another in an opposite direction in the farther side. The resulting effect is therefore only the difference of the two, and in the position as shown in the figure; this difference must be very small, since the opposite sides of the helix are approximately at the same distance from *c*. But the difference of action on the two sides constantly increases as the helix is brought near the side of the ring, and becomes a maximum when the two are in the position of internal contact. A helix of larger diameter would therefore produce a greater effect.

48. Coil No. 1 remaining as before, helix No. 1, which is nine inches in diameter, was substituted for the small helix of the last experiment, and with this the effect at a distance was much increased. When coil No. 2 was added to coil No. 1, and the currents from two small batteries sent through these, shocks were distinctly perceptible through the tongue, when the distance of the planes of the coils and the three helices, united as one, was increased to thirty-six inches.

49. The action at a distance was still further increased by coiling the long wire of the large spool into the form of a ring of four feet in diameter, and placing parallel to this another ring, formed of the four ribands of coils No. 1, 2, 3 and 4.   When a current from a single battery of thirty-five feet of zinc surface was passed through the riband conductor, shocks through the tongue were felt when the rings were separated to the distance of four feet.   As the conductors were approximated, the shocks became more and more severe; and when at the distance of twelve inches, they could not be taken through the body.

50. It may be stated in this connection, that the galvanic induction of magnetism in soft iron, in reference to distance, is also surprisingly great.   A cylinder of soft iron, two inches in diameter and one foot long, placed in the centre of the ring of copper riband, with the battery above mentioned, becomes strongly magnetic.

51. I may perhaps be excused for mentioning in this communication that the induction at a distance affords the means of exhibiting some of the most astonishing experiments, in the line of *physique amusante*, to be found perhaps in the whole course of science.   I will mention one which is somewhat connected with the experiments to be described in the next section, and which exhibits the action in a striking manner.   This consists in causing the induction to take place through the partition wall of two rooms.   For this purpose coil No. 1 is suspended against the wall in one room, while a person in the adjoining one receives the shock, by grasping the handles of the helix, and approaching it to the spot opposite to which the coil is suspended. The effect is as if by magic, without a visible cause.   It is best produced through a door, or thin wooden partition.

52. The action at a distance affords a simple method of graduating the intensity of the shock in the case of its application to medical purposes.   The helix may be suspended by a string passing over a pulley, and then gradually lowered down towards the plane of the coil, until the shocks are of the required intensity.   At the request of a medical friend, I have lately administered the induced current precisely in this way, in a case of paralysis of a part of the nerves of the face.

53. I may also mention that the energetic action of the spiral con-

VI.—4 D

ductors enables us to imitate, in a very striking manner, the inductive operation of the magneto-electrical machine, by means of an uninterrupted galvanic current. For this purpose it is only necessary to arrange two coils to represent the two poles of a horseshoe magnet, and to cause two helices to revolve past them in a parallel plane. While a constant current is passing through each coil, in opposite directions, the effect of the rotation of the helices is precisely the same as that of the revolving armature in the machine.

54. A remarkable fact should here be noted in reference to helix No. 4, which is connected with a subsequent part of the investigation. This helix is formed of copper wire, the spires of which are insulated by a coating of cement instead of thread, as in the case of the others. After being used in the above experiments, a small discharge from a Leyden jar was passed through it, and on applying it again to the coil, I was much surprised to find that scarcely any signs of a secondary current could be obtained.

55. The discharge had destroyed the insulation in some part, but this was not sufficient to prevent the magnetizing of a bar of iron introduced into the opening at the centre. The effect appeared to be confined to the inductive action. The same accident had before happened to another coil of nearly the same kind. It was therefore noted as one of some importance. An explanation was afterwards found in a peculiar action of the secondary current.

SECTION IV.

On the Effects produced by interposing different Substances between the Conductors.

56. Sir H. Davy found, in magnetizing needles by an electrical discharge, that the effect took place through interposed plates of all substances, conductors and nonconductors.* The experiment which I have given in paragraph 51 would appear to indicate that the inductive action which produces the secondary current might also follow the same law.

---

* Philosophical Transactions, 1821.

57. To test this the compound helix was placed about five inches above coil No. 1, Fig. 5, and a plate of sheet iron, about $\frac{1}{10}$th of an inch thick. interposed. With this arrangement no shocks could be obtained; although, when the plate was withdrawn, they were very intense.

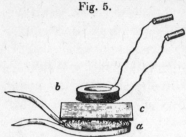

Fig. 5.

a represents coil No. 1, *b* helix No. 1, and *c* an interposed plate of metal.

58. It was at first thought that this effect might be peculiar to the iron, on account of its temporary magnetism; but this idea was shown to be erroneous by substituting a plate of zinc of about the same size and thickness. With this the screening influence was exhibited as before.

59. After this a variety of substances was interposed in succession, namely, copper, lead, mercury, acid, water, wood, glass, &c.; and it was found that all the perfect conductors, such as the metals, produced the screening influence; but nonconductors, as glass, wood, &c., appeared to have no effect whatever.

60. When the helix was separated from the coil by a distance only equal to the thickness of the plate, a slight sensation could be perceived even when the zinc of $\frac{1}{10}$th of an inch in thickness was interposed. This effect was increased by increasing the quantity of the battery current. If the thickness of the plate was diminished, the induction through it became more intense. Thus a sheet of tinfoil interposed produced no perceptible influence; also four sheets of the same were attended with the same result. A certain thickness of metal is therefore required to produce the screening effect, and this thickness depends on the quantity of the current from the battery.

61. The idea occurred to me that the screening might, in some way, be connected with an instantaneous current in the plate, similar to that in the induction by magnetic rotation, discovered by M. Arago. The ingenious variation of this principle by Messrs Babbage and Herschell, furnished me with a simple method of determining this point.

62. A circular plate of lead was interposed, which caused the induction in the helix almost entirely to disappear. A slip of the metal was then cut out in the direction of a radius of the circle, as is shown

Fig. 6. in Fig. 6. With the plate in this condition, no screening
was produced; the shocks were as intense as if the metal
were not present.

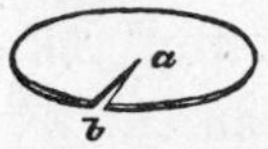

a represents a lead plate, of which the sector *b* is cut out.

63. This experiment however is not entirely satisfactory, since the action might have taken place through the opening of the lead; to obviate this objection, another plate was cut in the same manner, and the two interposed with a glass plate between them, and so arranged that the opening in the one might be covered by the continuous part of the other. Still shocks were obtained with undiminished intensity.

64. But the existence of a current in the interposed conductor was rendered certain by attaching the magnetizing spiral by means of two wires to the edge of the opening in the circular plate, as is shown in

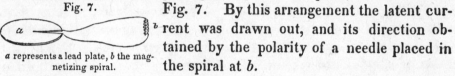

Fig. 7.

a represents a lead plate, *b* the magnetizing spiral.

Fig. 7. By this arrangement the latent current was drawn out, and its direction obtained by the polarity of a needle placed in the spiral at *b*.

65. This current was a secondary one, and its direction, in conformity with the discovery of Dr Faraday, was found to be the same as that of the primary current.

66. That the screening influence is in some way produced by the neutralizing action of the current thus obtained, will be clear, from the following experiment. The plate of zinc before mentioned, which is nearly twice the diameter of the helix, instead of being placed between the conductors, was put on the top of the helix, and in this position, although the neutralization was not as perfect as before, yet a great reduction was observed in the intensity of the shock.

67. But here a very interesting and puzzling question occurs. How does it happen that two currents, both in the same direction, can neutralize each other? I was at first disposed to consider the phenomenon as a case of real electrical interference, in which the impulses succeed each other by some regular interval. But if this were true the effect should depend on the length and other conditions of the current in the interposed conductor. In order to investigate this, several modifications of the experiments were instituted.

68. First a flat coil (No. 3) was interposed instead of the plates. When the two ends of this were separated, the shocks were received as if the coil were not present; but when the ends were joined, so as to form a perfect metallic circuit, no shocks could be obtained. The neutralization with the coil in this experiment was even more perfect than with the plate.

69. Again, coil No. 2, in the form of a ring, was placed not between the conductors, but around the helix. With this disposition of the apparatus, and the ends of the coil joined, the shocks were scarcely perceptible, but when the ends were separated, the presence of the coil has no effect.

70. Also when helix No. 1 and 2 were together submitted to the influence of coil No. 1, the ends of the one being joined, the other gave no shock.

71. The experiments were further varied by placing helix No. 2 within a hollow cylinder of sheet brass, and this again within coil No. 2 in a manner similar to that shown in Fig. 12, which is intended to illustrate another experiment. In this arrangement the neutralizing action was exhibited, as in the case of the plate.

72. A hollow cylinder of iron was next substituted for the one of brass, and with this also no shocks could be obtained.

73. From these experiments it is evident that the neutralization takes place with currents in the interposed or adjoining conductors of all lengths and intensities, and therefore cannot, as it appears to me, be referred to the interference of two systems of vibrations.

74. This part of the investigation was, for a time, given up almost in despair, and it was not until new light had been obtained from another part of the inquiry, that any further advances could be made towards a solution of the mystery.

In the remainder of this article, which we omit, Henry describes currents induced through chains of up to five pairs of separated coils, and the production of induced currents from the discharge of a Leyden jar. In conclusion he writes, "every part of the subject of electro-dynamic induction appears to open a field for discovery, which experimental industry cannot fail to cultivate with immediate success."

62

JOSEPH HENRY

ALBERT ABRAHAM MICHELSON

1852-1931

In the nineteenth century American professors' salaries would seldom support a dignified style of life, and to be a proper physics professor it was usually necessary to inherit wealth or marry it. It was less necessary to have a doctorate—as late as 1900 only a minority of professors had the Ph.D.—and physicists could set out with any sort of training. Albert A. Michelson's background, which seems odd to modern eyes, was not surprising in his own times.

Born in Strelno, Prussia (later Strzelno, Poland), son of a Jewish merchant, Michelson was brought to America as a small child. He grew up in the rough, booming mining towns of Murphy's Camp, California and Virginia City, Nevada. In 1869 he went to Annapolis as an appointee of President U. S. Grant. After graduation he stayed on at the Naval Academy as a science instructor.

A single event in November 1877 stamped a pattern on his life. While preparing a lecture demonstration of Foucault's method for determining the velocity of light, Michelson realized that if he collimated the beam he could get a much longer optical path-length and thus a great increase in sensitivity. In the next two years he did the experiment, aided by his enthusiasm and mechanical talent, and also by a grant from his father-in-law, amounting to $2000 (the equivalent of ten times as much today). Encouraged by success and by the advice of the prominent astronomer Simon Newcomb, Michelson resolved on a career in physics. He went to Europe for two years of study.

At Helmholtz's laboratory in Berlin Michelson designed and built a fundamental experiment. He had in mind a new sort of interferometer, sensitive enough to measure the second-order effects depending on the velocity of the earth's motion through the ether—that odd, stiff fluid which physicists of the day required as a medium to carry the vibrations of light. Michelson got a null result, and was disappointed. He felt that he had failed to measure the ether.

In 1882 he took a position at the Case School of Applied Science, the first of a series of positions at newly-founded science schools. He collaborated with the respected chemist Edward Morley in several researches, of which the most important was a repeat, now far more sensitive, of the Berlin experiment. Morley, a skilled experimentalist, made major contributions to the design and execution. The result was another discouraging "failure"; it seemed impossible to detect any motion through the ether. This experiment of Michelson and Morley was quickly recognized as the most striking and significant of several different kinds of attempts to measure the ether, which together prepared the ground of doubts and opinions among European physicists from which Einstein's theory of relativity sprang. Michelson later acknowledged the importance of Einstein's work, but to the end of his life he could never believe that light was not a vibration in some sort of ghostly ether.

In 1889 Michelson went to Clark University, and three years later moved on to become the head of the physics department at the University of Chicago, newly erected on a solid foundation of Rockefeller money. Both schools were struggling to guarantee scientists enough funds and time for pure research, while not neglecting education. As a teacher Michelson was aloof and forbidding, but lucid. In the course of his painstaking and exhausting researches and a difficult first marriage he had developed reserve and self-restraint. Still he was able to help physics teaching and research flourish at Chicago, and he was among the founders of The American Physical Society, becoming its second president.

For many years he labored to make diffraction gratings better than Henry Rowland's. But he was better known as the man who measured the International Meter in Paris against the wavelength of cadmium light; as the first American scientist to win a Nobel Prize (1907); and as the first person to measure the angular diameter of a star, which he did at the age of 67 with one of his beloved interferometers. His most sustained efforts went into surpassing his own classic measurements of the velocity of light. In 1926 he did this on a 22-mile baseline, within an uncertainty of ± 4 km sec^{-1}. Five years later he tried another measurement, now in an evacuated pipe a mile long, and died as he was writing up his results.

65

ALBERT ABRAHAM MICHELSON

In the nineteenth century, while physics lagged in the United States, American engineers and inventors had already become the equals or superiors of any in the world. American physicists felt the influence of this tradition, drawing on engineering and inventive skills in their pursuit of fundamental problems. The result can be seen in its most beautiful form in the Michelson-Morley apparatus, which managed to be at the same time ingenious and straightforward, massive and exquisitely delicate. The account that follows is from the *American Journal of Science* (vol. 35, 1887, p. 333-45).

No. 203. Vol. XXXIV. NOVEMBER, 1887.

Established by **BENJAMIN SILLIMAN** in 1818.

THE

AMERICAN

JOURNAL OF SCIENCE.

EDITORS

JAMES D. AND EDWARD S. DANA.

ASSOCIATE EDITORS

Professors ASA GRAY, JOSIAH P. COOKE, and JOHN TROWBRIDGE, of Cambridge,

Professors H. A. NEWTON and A. E. VERRILL, of New Haven,

Professor GEORGE F. BARKER, of Philadelphia.

THIRD SERIES.

VOL. XXXIV.—[WHOLE NUMBER, CXXXIV.]

WITH PLATES II TO IX.

No. 203—NOVEMBER, 1887.

NEW HAVEN, CONN.: J. D. & E. S. DANA.

1887.

TUTTLE, MOREHOUSE & TAYLOR, PRINTERS, 871 STATE STREET.

Six dollars per year (postage prepaid). $6.40 to foreign subscribers of countries in the Postal Union. Remittances should be made either by money orders, registered letters, or bank checks.

67

ALBERT ABRAHAM MICHELSON

THE

AMERICAN JOURNAL OF SCIENCE.

[THIRD SERIES.]

———•◦•———

ART. XXXVI.—*On the Relative Motion of the Earth and the Luminiferous Ether ;* by ALBERT A. MICHELSON and EDWARD W. MORLEY.*

THE discovery of the aberration of light was soon followed by an explanation according to the emission theory. The effect was attributed to a simple composition of the velocity of light with the velocity of the earth in its orbit. The difficulties in this apparently sufficient explanation were overlooked until after an explanation on the undulatory theory of light was proposed. This new explanation was at first almost as simple as the former. But it failed to account for the fact proved by experiment that the aberration was unchanged when observations were made with a telescope filled with water. For if the tangent of the angle of aberration is the ratio of the velocity of the earth to the velocity of light, then, since the latter velocity in water is three-fourths its velocity in a vacuum, the aberration observed with a water telescope should be four-thirds of its true value.†

* This research was carried out with the aid of the Bache Fund.

† It may be noticed that most writers admit the sufficiency of the explanation according to the emission theory of light; while in fact the difficulty is even greater than according to the undulatory theory. For on the emission theory the velocity of light must be greater in the water telescope, and therefore the angle of aberration should be less; hence, in order to reduce it to its true value, we must make the absurd hypothesis that the motion of the water in the telescope carries the ray of light in the opposite direction !

AM. JOUR. SCI.—THIRD SERIES, VOL. XXXIV, No. 203.—NOV., 1887.
22

On the undulatory theory, according to Fresnel, first, the ether is supposed to be at rest except in the interior of transparent media, in which secondly, it is supposed to move with a velociy less than the velocity of the medium in the ratio $\dfrac{n^2-1}{n^2}$, where n is the index of refraction. These two hypotheses give a complete and satisfactory explanation of aberration. The second hypothesis, notwithstanding its seeming improbability, must be considered as fully proved, first, by the celebrated experiment of Fizeau,* and secondly, by the ample confirmation of our own work.† The experimental trial of the first hypothesis forms the subject of the present paper.

If the earth were a transparent body, it might perhaps be conceded, in view of the experiments just cited, that the intermolecular ether was at rest in space, notwithstanding the motion of the earth in its orbit; but we have no right to extend the conclusion from these experiments to opaque bodies. But there can hardly be question that the ether can and does pass through metals. Lorentz cites the illustration of a metallic barometer tube. When the tube is inclined the ether in the space above the mercury is certainly forced out, for it is incompressible.‡ But again we have no right to assume that it makes its escape with perfect freedom, and if there be any resistance, however slight, we certainly could not assume an opaque body such as the whole earth to offer free passage through its entire mass. But as Lorentz aptly remarks: "quoi qui'l en soit, on fera bien, à mon avis, de ne pas se laisser guider, dans une question aussi importante, par des considérations sur le degré de probabilité ou de simplicité de l'une ou de l'autre hypothèse, mais de s'addresser a l'expérience pour apprendre à connaitre l'état, de repos ou de mouvement, dans lequel se trouve l'éther à la surface terrestre."§

In April, 1881, a method was proposed and carried out for testing the question experimentally.‖

In deducing the formula for the quantity to be measured, the effect of the motion of the earth through the ether on the path of the ray at right angles to this motion was overlooked.¶

* Comptes Rendus, xxxiii, 349, 1851; Pogg. Ann. Ergänzungsband, iii, 457, 1853; Ann. Chim. Phys., III, lvii, 385, 1859.

† Influence of Motion of the Medium on the Velocity of Light. This Journal, III, xxxi, 377, 1886.

‡ It may be objected that it may escape by the space between the mercury and the walls; but this could be prevented by amalgamating the walls.

§ Archives Néerlandaises, xxi, 2ᵐᵉ livr.

‖ The relative motion of the earth and the luminiferous ether, by Albert A. Michelson, this Jour., III, xxii, 120.

¶ It may be mentioned here that the error was pointed out to the author of the former paper by M. A. Potier, of Paris, in the winter of 1881.

ALBERT ABRAHAM MICHELSON

The discusssion of this oversight and of the entire experiment forms the subject of a very searching analysis by H. A. Lorentz,* who finds that this effect can by no means be disregarded. In consequence, the quantity to be measured had in fact but one-half the value supposed, and as it was already barely beyond the limits of errors of experiment, the conclusion drawn from the result of the experiment might well be questioned; since, however, the main portion of the theory remains unquestioned, it was decided to repeat the experiment with such modifications as would insure a theoretical result much too large to be masked by experimental errors. The theory of the method may be briefly stated as follows:

Let *sa*, fig. 1, be a ray of light which is partly reflected in *ab*, and partly transmitted in *ac*, being returned by the mirrors *b* and *c*, along *ba* and *ca*. *ba* is partly transmitted along *ad*,

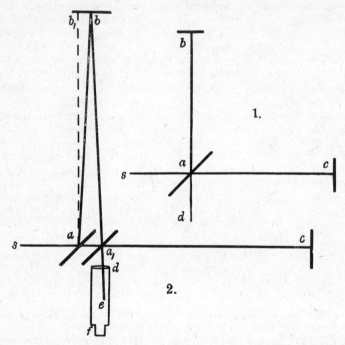

and *ca* is partly reflected along *ad*. If then the paths *ab* and *ac* are equal, the two rays interfere along *ad*. Suppose now, the ether being at rest, that the whole apparatus moves in the direction *sc*, with the velocity of the earth in its orbit, the direc-

* De l'Influence du Mouvement de la Terre sur les Phen. Lum. Archives Néerlandaises, xxi, 2ᵐᵉ livr., 1886.

tions and distances traversed by the rays will be altered thus :—
The ray sa is reflected along ab, fig. 2; the angle bab, being
equal to the aberration $=a$, is returned along $ba_{,,}$ $(aba_{,} =2a)$, and
goes to the focus of the telescope, whose direction is unaltered.
The transmitted ray goes along ac, is returned along $ca_{,,}$ and is
reflected at $a_{,}$ making $ca_{,}e$ equal $90-a$, and therefore still coin-
ciding with the first ray. It may be remarked that the rays $ba_{,}$
and $ca_{,,}$ do not now meet exactly in the same point $a_{,,}$ though
the difference is of the second order ; this does not affect the
validity of the reasoning. Let it now be required to find the
difference in the two paths $aba_{,}$ and $aca_{,}$.
Let $V=$ velocity of light.
$\qquad v=$ velocity of the earth in its orbit.
$\qquad D=$ distance ab or ac, fig. 1.
$\qquad T=$ time light occupies to pass from a to c.
$\qquad T=$ time light occupies to return from c to $a_{,}$, (fig. 2.)

Then $T=\dfrac{D}{V-v}$, $T_{,}=\dfrac{D}{V+v}$. The whole time of going and com-

ing is $T+T_{,}=2D\dfrac{V}{V^2-v^2}$, and the distance traveled in this time

is $2D\dfrac{V^2}{V^2-v^2}=2D\left(1+\dfrac{v^2}{V^2}\right)$, neglecting terms of the fourth order.

The length of the other path is evidently $2D\sqrt{1+\dfrac{v^2}{V^2}}$, or to the

same degree of accuracy, $2D\left(1+\dfrac{v^2}{2V^2}\right)$. The difference is there-

fore $D\dfrac{v^2}{V^2}$. If now the whole apparatus be turned through 90°,

the difference will be in the opposite direction, hence the dis-

placement of the interference fringes should be $2D\dfrac{v^2}{V^2}$. Con-

sidering only the velocity of the earth in its orbit, this would
be $2D\times10^{-8}$. If, as was the case in the first experiment,
$D=2\times10^6$ waves of yellow light, the displacement to be
expected would be 0·04 of the distance between the interference
fringes.
   In the first experiment one of the principal difficulties en-
countered was that of revolving the apparatus without producing distortion ; and another was its extreme sensitiveness to
vibration. This was so great that it was impossible to see the
interference fringes except at brief intervals when working in
the city, even at two o'clock in the morning. Finally, as before remarked, the quantity to be observed, namely, a displacement of something less than a twentieth of the distance between the interference fringes may have been too small to be
detected when masked by experimental errors.

ALBERT ABRAHAM MICHELSON

The first named difficulties were entirely overcome by mounting the apparatus on a massive stone floating on mercury ; and the second by increasing, by repeated reflection, the path of the light to about ten times its former value.

The apparatus is represented in perspective in fig. 3, in plan in fig. 4, and in vertical section in fig. 5. The stone *a* (fig. 5) is about 1·5 meter square and 0·3 meter thick. It rests on an annular wooden float *bb*, 1·5 meter outside diameter, 0·7 meter inside diameter, and 0·25 meter thick. The float rests on mercury contained in the cast-iron trough *cc*, 1·5 centimeter thick, and of such dimensions as to leave a clearance of about one centimeter around the float. A pin *d*, guided by arms *gggg*, fits into a socket *e* attached to the float. The pin may be pushed into the socket or be withdrawn, by a lever pivoted at *f*. This pin keeps the float concentric with the trough, but does not bear any part of the weight of the stone. The annular iron trough rests on a bed of cement on a low brick pier built in the form of a hollow octagon.

3.

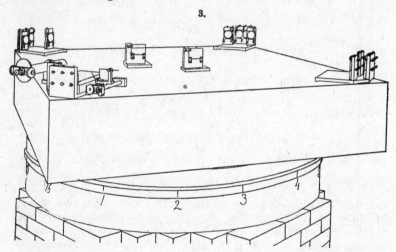

At each corner of the stone were placed four mirrors *dd ee* fig. 4. Near the center of the stone was a plane-parallel glass *b*. These were so disposed that light from an argand burner *a*, passing through a lens, fell on *b* so as to be in part reflected to *d₁*; the two pencils followed the paths indicated in the figure, *bdedbf* and *bd,e,d,bf* respectively, and were observed by the telescope *f*. Both *f* and *a* revolved with the stone. The mirrors were of speculum metal carefully worked to optically plane surfaces five centimeters in diameter, and the glasses *b* and *c* were plane-parallel and of the same thickness. 1·25 centimeter ;

their surfaces measured 5·0 by 7·5 centimeters. The second of these was placed in the path of one of the pencils to compensate for the passage of the other through the same thickness of glass. The whole of the optical portion of the apparatus was kept covered with a wooden cover to prevent air currents and rapid changes of temperature.

The adjustment was effected as follows: The mirrors having been adjusted by screws in the castings which held the

4.

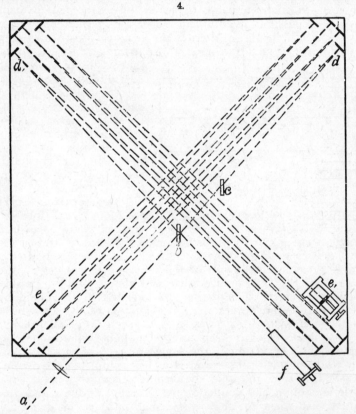

mirrors, against which they were pressed by springs, till light from both pencils could be seen in the telescope, the lengths of the two paths were measured by a light wooden rod reaching diagonally from mirror to mirror, the distance being read from a small steel scale to tenths of millimeters. The difference in the lengths of the two paths was then annulled by moving the mirror $e_{,}$. This mirror had three adjustments; it had an adjustment in altitude and one in azimuth, like all the other mirrors, but finer ; it also had an adjustment in the direction of the incident ray, sliding forward or backward, but keeping very accurately parallel to its former plane. The three adjustments of this mirror could be made with the wooden cover in position.

The paths being now approximately equal, the two images of the source of light or of some well-defined object placed in front of the condensing lens, were made to coincide, the telescope was now adjusted for distinct vision of the expected interference bands, and sodium light was substituted for white light, when the interference bands appeared. These were now made as clear as possible by adjusting the mirror e_i; then white light was restored, the screw altering the length of path was very slowly moved (one turn of a screw of one hundred threads to the inch altering the path nearly 1000 wave-lengths) till the colored interference fringes reappeared in white light. These were now given a convenient width and position, and the apparatus was ready for observation.

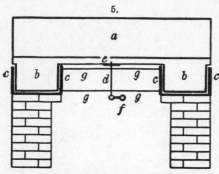

The observations were conducted as follows : Around the cast-iron trough were sixteen equidistant marks. The apparatus was revolved very slowly (one turn in six minutes) and after a few minutes the cross wire of the micrometer was set on the clearest of the interference fringes at the instant of passing one of the marks. The motion was so slow that this could be done readily and accurately. The reading of the screw-head on the micrometer was noted, and a very slight and gradual impulse was given to keep up the motion of the stone ; on passing the second mark, the same process was repeated, and this was continued till the apparatus had completed six revolutions. It was found that by keeping the apparatus in slow uniform motion, the results were much more uniform and consistent than when the stone was brought to rest for every observation ; for the effects of strains could be noted for at least half a minute after the stone came to rest, and during this time effects of change of temperature came into action.

The following tables give the means of the six readings ; the first, for observations made near noon, the second, those near six o'clock in the evening. The readings are divisions of the screw-heads. The width of the fringes varied from 40 to 60 divisions, the mean value being near 50, so that one division means 0·02 wave-length. The rotation in the observations at noon was contrary to, and in the evening observations, with, that of the hands of a watch.

Noon Observations.

	16.	1.	2.	3.	4.	5.	6.	7.	8.	9.	10.	11.	12.	13.	14.	15.	16·
July 8	44·7	44·0	43·5	39·7	35·2	34·7	34·3	32·5	28·2	26·2	23·8	23·2	20·3	18·7	17·5	16·8	13·7
July 9	57·4	57·3	58·2	59·2	58·7	60·2	60·8	62·0	61·5	63·3	65·8	67·3	69·7	70·7	73·0	70·2	72·2
July 11	27·3	23·5	22·0	19·3	19·2	19·3	18·7	18·8	16·2	14·3	13·3	12·8	13·3	12·3	10·2	7·3	6·5
Mean........	43·1	41·6	41·2	39·4	37·7	38·1	37·9	37·8	35·3	34·6	34·3	34·4	34·4	33·9	33·6	31·4	30·8
Mean in w. l.	·862	·832	·824	·788	·754	·762	·758	·756	·706	·692	·686	·688	·688	·678	·672	·628	·616
	·706	·692	·686	·688	·688	·678	·672	·628	·616								
Final mean.	·784	·762	·755	·738	·721	·720	·715	·692	·661								

P. M. Observations.

	16.	1.	2.	3.	4.	5.	6.	7.	8.	9.	10.	11.	12.	13.	14.	15.	16·
July 8	61·2	63·3	63·3	68·2	67·7	69·3	70·3	69·8	69·0	71·3	71·3	70·5	71·2	71·2	70·5	72·5	75·7
July 9	26·0	26·0	28·2	29·2	31·5	32·0	31·3	31·7	33·0	35·8	36·5	37·3	38·8	41·0	42·7	43·7	44·0
July 12	66·8	66·5	66·0	64·3	62·2	61·0	61·3	59·7	58·2	55·7	53·7	54·7	55·0	58·2	58·5	57·0	56·0
Mean	51·3	51·9	52·5	53·9	53·8	54·1	54·3	53·7	53·4	54·3	53·8	54·2	55·0	56·8	57·2	57·7	58·6
Mean in w. l.	1·026	1·038	1·050	1·078	1·076	1·082	1·086	1·074	1·068	1·086	1·076	1·084	1·100	1·136	1·144	1·154	1·172
	1·068	1·086	1·076	1·084	1·100	1·136	1·144	1·154	1·172								
Final mean.	1·047	1·062	1·063	1·081	1·088	1·109	1·115	1·114	1·120								

The results of the observations are expressed graphically in fig. 6. The upper is the curve for the observations at noon, and the lower that for the evening observations. The dotted curves represent *one-eighth* of the theoretical displacements. It seems fair to conclude from the figure that if there is any dis-

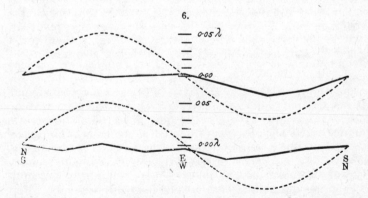

6.

placement due to the relative motion of the earth and the luminiferous ether, this cannot be much greater than 0·01 of the distance between the fringes.

Considering the motion of the earth in its orbit only, this

ALBERT ABRAHAM MICHELSON

displacement should be $2D\dfrac{v^2}{V^2}=2D\times10^{-8}$. The distance D was about eleven meters, or 2×10^7 wave-lengths of yellow light; hence the displacement to be expected was 0·4 fringe. The actual displacement was certainly less than the twentieth part of this, and probably less than the fortieth part. But since the displacement is proportional to the square of the velocity, the relative velocity of the earth and the ether is probably less than one sixth the earth's orbital velocity, and certainly less than one-fourth.

In what precedes, only the orbital motion of the earth is considered. If this is combined with the motion of the solar system, concerning which but little is known with certainty, the result would have to be modified; and it is just possible that the resultant velocity at the time of the observations was small though the chances are much against it. The experiment will therefore be repeated at intervals of three months, and thus all uncertainty will be avoided.

It appears, from all that precedes, reasonably certain that if there be any relative motion between the earth and the luminiferous ether, it must be small; quite small enough entirely to refute Fresnel's explanation of aberration. Stokes has given a theory of aberration which assumes the ether at the earth's surface to be at rest with regard to the latter, and only requires in addition that the relative velocity have a potential; but Lorentz shows that these conditions are incompatible. Lorentz then proposes a modification which combines some ideas of Stokes and Fresnel, and assumes the existence of a potential, together with Fresnel's coefficient. If now it were legitimate to conclude from the present work that the ether is at rest with regard to the earth's surface, according to Lorentz there could not be a velocity potential, and his own theory also fails.

Supplement.

It is obvious from what has gone before that it would be hopeless to attempt to solve the question of the motion of the solar system by observations of optical phenomena *at the surface of the earth.* But it is not impossible that at even moderate distances above the level of the sea, at the top of an isolated mountain peak, for instance, the relative motion might be perceptible in an apparatus like that used in these experiments. Perhaps if the experiment should ever be tried in these circumstances, the cover should be of glass, or should be removed.

It may be worth while to notice another method for multiplying the square of the aberration sufficiently to bring it within the range of observation, which has presented itself during the

76

ALBERT ABRAHAM MICHELSON

preparation of this paper. This is founded on the fact that reflection from surfaces in motion varies from the ordinary laws of reflection.

Let ab (fig. 1) be a plane wave falling on the mirror mn at an incidence of 45°. If the mirror is at rest, the wave front after reflection will be ac.

Now suppose the mirror to move in a direction which makes an angle a with its normal, with a velocity ω. Let V be the velocity of light in the ether supposed stationary, and let cd be the increase in the distance the light has to travel to reach d. In this time the mirror will have moved a distance $\dfrac{cd}{\sqrt{2}\cos a}$.

We have $\dfrac{cd}{ad} = \dfrac{\omega\sqrt{2}\cos a}{V}$ which put $= r$, and $\dfrac{ac}{ad} = 1-r$.

In order to find the new wave front, draw the arc fg with b as a center and ad as radius; the tangent to this arc from d will be the new wave front, and the normal to the tangent from b will be the new direction. This will differ from the direction ba by the angle θ which it is required to find. From the equality of the triangles adb and edb it follows that $\theta = 2\varphi$, $ab = ac$,

$$\tan adb = \tan\left(45° - \frac{\theta}{2}\right) = \frac{1-\tan\dfrac{\theta}{2}}{1+\tan\dfrac{\theta}{2}} = \frac{ac}{ad} = 1-r,$$

or neglecting terms of the order r^3,

$$\theta = r + \frac{r^2}{2} = \frac{\sqrt{2}\omega\cos a}{V} + \frac{\omega^2}{V^2}\cos^2 a.$$

Now let the light fall on a parallel mirror facing the first, we should then have $\theta_{\prime} = \dfrac{-\sqrt{2}\omega\cos a}{V} + \dfrac{\omega^2}{V^2}\cos^2 a$, and the total deviation would be $\theta + \theta_{\prime} = 2\rho^2\cos^2 a$ where ρ is the angle of aberration, if only the orbital motion of the earth is considered. The maximum displacement obtained by revolving the whole apparatus through 90° would be $\varDelta = 2\rho^2 = 0\cdot004''$. With fifty such couples the displacement would be $0\cdot2''$. But astronomical observations in circumstances far less favorable than those in which these may be taken have been made to hundredths of a second; so that this new method bids fair to be at least as sensitive as the former.

The arrangement of apparatus might be as in fig. 2; s in the focus of the lens a, is a slit; bb cc are two glass mirrors optically plane and so silvered as to allow say one-twentieth of the light to pass through, and reflecting say ninety per cent. The intensity of the light falling on the observing telescope df

ALBERT ABRAHAM MICHELSON

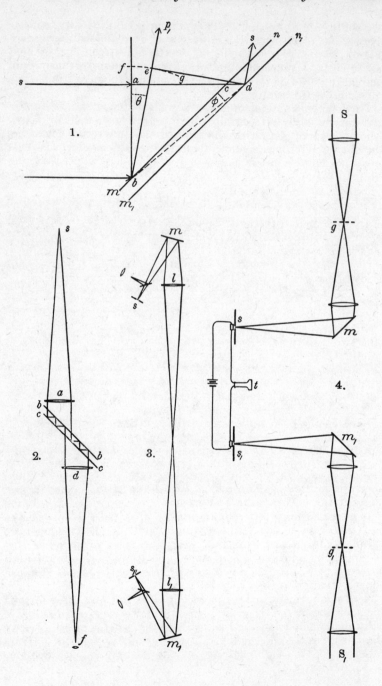

1.

2.

3.

4.

would be about one-millionth of the original intensity, so that if sunlight or the electric arc were used it could still be readily seen. The mirrors bb, and cc, would differ from parallelism sufficiently to separate the successive images. Finally, the apparatus need not be mounted so as to revolve, as the earth's rotation would be sufficient.

If it were possible to measure with sufficient accuracy the velocity of light without returning the ray to its starting point, the problem of measuring the first power of the relative velocity of the earth with respect to the ether would be solved. This may not be as hopeless as might appear at first sight, since the difficulties are entirely mechanical and may possibly be surmounted in the course of time.

For example, suppose (fig. 3) m and m, two mirrors revolving with equal velocity in opposite directions. It is evident that light from s will form a stationary image at s, and similarly light from s, will form a stationary image at s. If now the velocity of the mirrors be increased sufficiently, their phases still being exactly the same, both images will be deflected from s and s, in inverse proportion to the velocities of light in the two directions; or, if the two deflections are made equal, and the difference of phase of the mirrors be simultaneously measured, this will evidently be proportional to the difference of velocity in the two directions. The only real difficulty lies in this measurement. The following is perhaps a possible solution : gg, (fig. 4) are two gratings on which sunlight is concentrated. These are placed so that after falling on the revolving mirrors m and m, the light forms images of the gratings at s and s, two very sensitive selenium cells in circuit with a battery and a telephone. If everything be symmetrical, the sound in the telephone will be a maximum. If now one of the slits s be displaced through half the distance between the image of the grating bars, there will be silence. Suppose now that the two deflections having been made exactly equal, the slit is adjusted for silence. Then if the experiment be repeated when the earth's rotation has turned the whole apparatus through 180°, and the deflections are again made equal, there will no longer be silence, and the angular distance through which s must be moved to restore silence will measure the required difference in phase.

There remain three other methods, all astronomical, for attacking the problem of the motion of the solar system through space.

1. The telescopic observation of the proper motions of the stars. This has given us a highly probably determination of the direction of this motion, but only a guess as to its amount.

2. The spectroscopic observation of the motion of stars in the line of sight. This could furnish data for the relative

ALBERT ABRAHAM MICHELSON

motions only, though it seems likely that by the immense improvements in the photography of stellar spectra, the information thus obtained will be far more accurate than any other.

3. Finally there remains the determination of the velocity of light by observations of the eclipses of Jupiter's satellites. If the improved photometric methods practiced at the Harvard observatory make it possible to observe these with sufficient accuracy, the difference in the results found for the velocity of light when Jupiter is nearest to and farthest from the line of motion will give, not merely the motion of the solar system with reference to the stars, but with reference to the luminiferous ether itself.

HENRY AUGUSTUS ROWLAND

1848-1901

Once when **Henry Rowland** was involved in a lawsuit, the court noted the fact that he was "the highest known authority in this country upon the subject of the laws and principles of electricity . . . " From this incident there grew a legend that Rowland had declared under oath that he was the world's greatest physicist. Like many apocryphal tales about scientists, this one symbolizes a truth: some American physicists were growing self-confident as the nineteenth century ended. After long struggle they had finally won to a high level of excellence.

None struggled harder than Rowland. His boyhood and youth were spent in impassioned efforts to find the means and the freedom for fundamental research. He came from a long line of sturdy Protestant theologians (his great-grandfather had spoken from his pulpit against foreign oppression so zealously that during the War for Independence, when a British fleet invested Providence, he had to flee the city). Henry Rowland was expected to go into the ministry, but he preferred to work on home-made experiments. He rebelled so strongly against education in the classics that his family gave in, and at the age of seventeen he was sent to Rensselaer Technological Institute. He graduated in 1870 as a civil engineer and after two years in unsatisfactory jobs returned to Rensselaer as instructor in natural philosophy.

Whatever time he could spare from teaching he spent in research on magnetic permeability. His report on his work was rejected by the *American Journal of Science*, so he sent it to James Maxwell in Britain; Maxwell, impressed, had it published in London in the *Philosophical Magazine*. Few people in the United States noticed the paper. Rowland grew increasingly disgusted with his situation at Rensselaer and with the difficulties of physics research in America generally. Later, in 1883, he told a meeting of the American

Association for the Advancement of Science, "I here assert that all *can* find time for scientific research if they desire it. But here, again, that curse of our country, mediocrity, is upon us. Our colleges and universities seldom call for first-class men of reputation, and I have even heard the trustee of a well-known college assert that no professor should engage in research because of the time wasted."

Rowland's quest for a place to do research ended suddenly in 1875 when he met Daniel Coit Gilman. Gilman was assembling a faculty for the newly endowed Johns Hopkins University, which was to be America's first true research institution, complete with graduate students, on the German model. Rowland joined happily and was sent on a tour of Europe to study laboratories and buy instruments. At Helmoltz's laboratory in Berlin, Rowland (like Michelson five years later) paused to perform a fundamental experiment which he had conceived earlier but had lacked the means to perform. This was a search for the magnetic effect of a charged rotating disc, a matter of considerable interest at a time when Maxwell's equations were the subject of vigorous debate. The experiment was difficult in the extreme, demanding extensive mathematical calculations as well as measurements at the edge of detectability, but Rowland carried it off. His work, the first demonstration that a charged body in motion produces a magnetic field, attracted much attention.

Rowland returned to Johns Hopkins with one of the finest collections of research instruments in the world. At the university he gave as little attention as possible to administration and teaching. To his students and colleagues he was often a forbidding figure, intolerant of mediocrity, so devoted to the truth that his frank criticism could be devastating. He spent most of the 1870's and 1880's in his laboratory turning out a remarkably varied and competent series of researches.

Although he was a capable mathematician and did some work on electromagnetic theory, Rowland's true genius was for experiment. He determined authoritatively the absolute value of the Ohm, the ratio of electrical units, the mechanical equivalent of heat, and the variation (which he was the first to demonstrate) of the specific heat of water with temperature. He also suggested and supervised the experiments which led one of his graduate students to the discovery of the Hall effect. But his greatest contribution to science was the construction of diffraction gratings, begun in 1882. Rowland's gratings were more than an order of magnitude larger and more accurate than any previous ones. He also discovered the peculiar advantages of ruling a grating on a concave surface. He sold hundreds of his plane and concave gratings at cost, and for a generation they were the foundation of physical, chemical and astronomical spectroscopy around the world. Rowland himself used his gratings to prepare a classic map of the solar spectrum.

Rowland married in 1890 and soon after learned that he was dying of diabetes. To provide for his family he devoted himself to inventing and patenting improvements in telegraphy. He wished to leave something for physics, too, and towards his death he was one of the principal founders and first president of The American Physical Society.

Rather than give one of Rowland's many excellent and elaborate scientific papers, we have chosen his description of the simple mechanical device with which he revolutionized spectroscopy, from the *Encyclopedia Brittanica* (9th ed., p. 552-53, reprinted here from *The Physical Papers of Henry Rowland*, 1902). We also give his famous address to The American Physical Society, reproduced from the first number of the Society's *Bulletin* (1899). It presents an overview of physics on the eve of the revolutions of quantum mechanics and relativity, and also gives an overview of the physicist himself. Today Rowland's image may seem almost arrogant in its élitism—but it was such feelings that raised American physics to a high professional level.

SCREW

[*Encyclopædia Britannica, Ninth Edition, Volume XXI*]

The screw is the simplest instrument for converting a uniform motion of rotation into a uniform motion of translation (see ' Mechanics,' vol. xv, p. 754). Metal screws requiring no special accuracy are generally cut by taps and dies. A tap is a cylindrical piece of steel having a screw on its exterior with sharp cutting edges; by forcing this with a revolving motion into a hole of the proper size, a screw is cut on its interior forming what is known as a nut or female screw. The die is a nut with sharp cutting edges used to screw upon the outside of round pieces of metal and thus produce male screws. More accurate screws are cut in a lathe by causing the carriage carrying the tool to move uniformly forward, thus a continuous spiral line is cut on the uniformly revolving cylinder fixed between the lathe centres. The cutting tool may be an ordinary form of lathe tool or a revolving saw-like disk (see ' Machine Tools,' vol. xv, p. 153).

Errors of Screws.—For scientific purposes the screw must be so regular that it moves forward in its nut exactly the same distance for each given angular rotation around its axis. As the mountings of a screw introduce many errors, the final and exact test of its accuracy can only be made when it is finished and set up for use. A large screw can, however, be roughly examined in the following manner: (1) See whether the surface of the threads has a perfect polish. The more it departs from this, and approaches the rough, torn surface as cut by the lathe tool, the worse it is. A perfect screw has a perfect polish. (2) Mount upon it between the centres of a lathe and the slip a short nut which fits perfectly. If the nut moves from end to end with equal friction, the screw is uniform in diameter. If the nut is long, unequal resistance may be due to either an error of run or a bend in the screw. (3) Fix a microscope on the lathe carriage and focus its single cross-hair on the edge of the screw and parallel to its axis. If the screw runs true at every point, its axis is straight. (4) Observe whether the short nut runs from end to end of the screw without a wabbling motion when the screw is turned and the nut kept from revolving. If it wabbles the

HENRY AUGUSTUS ROWLAND

screw is said to be drunk. One can see this error better by fixing a long pointer to the nut, or by attaching to it a mirror and observing an image in it with a telescope. The following experiment will also detect this error: (5) Put upon the screw two well-fitting and rather short nuts, which are kept from revolving by arms bearing against a straight edge parallel to the axis of the screw. Let one nut carry an arm which supports a microscope focused on a line ruled on the other nut. Screw this combination to different parts of the screw. If during one revolution the microscope remains in focus, the screw is not drunk; and if the cross-hairs bisect the lines in every position, there is no error of run.

Making Accurate Screws.—To produce a screw of a foot or even a yard long with errors not exceeding $\frac{1}{1000}$th of an inch is not difficult. Prof. Wm. A. Rogers, of Harvard Observatory, has invented a process in which the tool of the lathe while cutting the screw is moved so as to counteract the errors of the lathe screw. The screw is then partly ground to get rid of local errors. But, where the highest accuracy is needed, we must resort in the case of screws, as in all other cases, to grinding. A long, solid nut, tightly fitting the screw in one position, cannot be moved freely to another position unless the screw is very accurate. If grinding material is applied and the nut is constantly tightened, it will grind out all errors of run, drunkenness, crookedness, and irregularity of size. The condition is that the nut must be long, rigid and capable of being tightened as the grinding proceeds; also the screw must be ground longer than it will finally be needed so that the imperfect ends may be removed.

The following process will produce a screw suitable for ruling gratings for optical purposes. Suppose it is our purpose to produce a screw which is finally to be 9 inches long, not including bearings, and $1\frac{1}{8}$ in. in diameter. Select a bar of soft Bessemer steel, which has not the hard spots usually found in cast steel, and about $1\frac{3}{8}$ inches in diameter and 30 long. Put it between lathe centres and turn it down to one inch diameter everywhere, except about 12 inches in the centre, where it is left a little over $1\frac{1}{8}$ inches in diameter for cutting the screw. Now cut the screw with a triangular thread a little sharper than 60°. Above all, avoid a fine screw, using about 20 threads to the inch.

The grinding nut, about 11 inches long, has now to be made. Fig. 1 represents a section of the nut, which is made of brass, or better, of Bessemer steel. It consists of four segments,—*a, a,* which can be drawn about the screw by two collars, *b, b,* and the screw *c.* Wedges between

86

HENRY AUGUSTUS ROWLAND

the segments prevent too great pressure on the screw. The final clamping is effected by the rings and screws, *d, d*, which enclose the flanges, *e*, of the segments. The screw is now placed in a lathe and surrounded by water whose temperature can be kept constant to 1° C., and the nut placed on it. In order that the weight of the nut may not make the ends too small, it must either be counterbalanced by weights hung from a rope passing over pulleys in the ceiling, or the screw must be vertical during the whole process. Emery and oil seem to be the only available grinding materials, though a softer silica powder might be used towards the end of the operation to clean off the emery and prevent future wear. Now grind the screw in the nut, making the nut pass backwards and forwards over the screw, its whole range being nearly 20 inches at first.

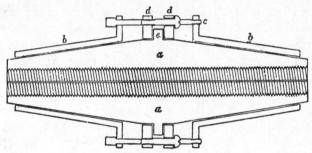

FIG. 1.—Section of Grinding Nut.

Turn the nut end for end every ten minutes and continue for two weeks, finally making the range of the nut only about 10 inches, using finer washed emery and moving the lathe slower to avoid heating. Finish with a fine silica powder or rouge. During the process, if the thread becomes too blunt, recut the nut by a *short* tap so as not to change the pitch at any point. This must, of course, not be done less than five days before the finish. Now cut to the proper length; centre again in the lathe under a microscope, and turn the bearings. A screw so ground has less errors than from any other system of mounting. The periodic error especially will be too small to be discovered, though the mountings and graduation and centering of the head will introduce it; it must therefore finally be corrected.

Mounting of Screws.—The mounting must be devised most carefully, and is, indeed, more difficult to make without error than the screw itself. The principle which should be adopted is that no workmanship is perfect; the design must make up for its imperfections. Thus the screw can never be made to run true on its bearings, and hence the device of resting one end of the carriage on the nut must be rejected. Also all rigid connection between the nut and the carriage must be avoided, as the screw can never be adjusted parallel to the ways on which the carriage rests. For many purposes, such as ruling optical gratings, the carriage must move accurately forward in a straight line as far as the horizontal plane is concerned, while a little curvature in the vertical plane produces very little effect. These conditions can be satisfied by making the ways V-shaped and grinding with a grinder somewhat shorter than the ways. By constant reversals and by lengthening or shortening the stroke, they will finally become nearly perfect. The vertical curvature can be sufficiently tested by a short carriage carrying a delicate spirit level. Another and very efficient form of ways is V-shaped with a flat top and nearly vertical sides. The carriage rests on the flat top and is held by springs against one of the nearly vertical sides. To determine with accuracy whether the ways are straight, fix a flat piece of glass on the carriage and rule a line on it by moving it under a diamond; reverse and rule another line near the first, and measure the distance apart at the centre and at the two ends by a micrometer. If the centre measurement is equal to the mean of the two end ones, the line is straight. This is better than the method with a mirror mounted on the carriage and a telescope. The screw itself must rest in bearings, and the end motion be prevented by a point bearing against its flat end, which is protected by hardened steel or a flat diamond. Collar bearings introduce periodic errors. The secret of success is so to design the nut and its connections as to eliminate all adjustments of the screw and indeed all imperfect workmanship. The connection must also be such as to give means of correcting any residual periodic errors or errors of run which may be introduced in the mountings or by the wear of the machine.

The nut is shown in Fig 2. It is made in two halves, of wrought iron filled with boxwood or lignum vitae plugs, on which the screw is cut. To each half a long piece of sheet steel is fixed which bears against a guiding edge, to be described presently. The two halves are held to the screw by springs, so that each moves forward almost independently of the other. To join the nut to the carriage, a ring is attached to the latter, whose plane is vertical and which can turn round a vertical axis. The bars fixed midway on the two halves of the nut bear against this ring at points 90° distant from its axis. Hence each half does its share independently of the other in moving the carriage forward. Any want

HENRY AUGUSTUS ROWLAND

of parallelism between the screws and the ways or eccentricity in the screw mountings thus scarcely affects the forward motion of the carriage. The guide against which the steel pieces of the nut rest can be made of such form as to correct any small error of run due to wear of the screw. Also, by causing it to move backwards and forwards periodically, the periodic error of the head and mountings can be corrected.

In making gratings for optical purposes the periodic error must be very perfectly eliminated, since the periodic displacement of the lines only one-millionth of an inch from their mean position will produce

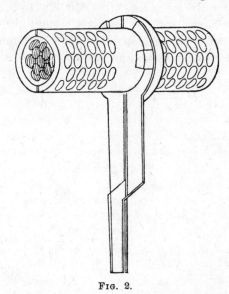

Fig. 2.

" ghosts " in the spectrum.[1] Indeed, this is the most sensitive method of detecting the existence of this error, and it is practically impossible to mount the most perfect of screws without introducing it. A very practical method of determining this error is to rule a short grating with very long lines on a piece of common thin plate glass; cut it in two with a diamond and superimpose the two halves with the rulings together and displaced sideways over each other one-half the pitch of the screw. On now looking at the plates in a proper light so as to have the spec-

---

[1] In a machine made by the present writer for ruling gratings the periodic error is entirely due to the graduation and centering of the head. The uncorrected periodic error from this cause displaces the lines $\frac{1}{300000}$th of an inch, which is sufficient to entirely ruin all gratings made without correcting it.

tral colors show through it, dark lines will appear, which are wavy if there is a periodic error and straight if there is none. By measuring the comparative amplitude of the waves and the distance apart of the two lines, the amount of the periodic error can be determined. The phase of the periodic error is best found by a series of trials after setting the corrector at the proper amplitude as determined above.

A machine properly made as above and kept at a constant temperature should be able to make a scale of 6 inches in length, with errors at no point exceeding $\frac{1}{100000}$th of an inch. When, however, a grating of that length is attempted at the rate of 14,000 lines to the inch, four days and nights are required, and the result is seldom perfect, possibly on account of the wear of the machine or changes of temperature. Gratings, however, less than 3 inches long are easy to make.

HENRY AUGUSTUS ROWLAND

THE HIGHEST AIM OF THE PHYSICIST.

BY HENRY A. ROWLAND.

[PRESIDENTIAL ADDRESS DELIVERED AT THE SECOND MEETING OF THE SOCIETY, ON OCTOBER 28, 1899.]

Gentlemen and Fellow Physicists of America :

We meet to-day on an occasion which marks an epoch in the history of physics in America ; may the future show that it also marks an epoch in the history of the science which this society is organized to cultivate ! For we meet here in the interest of a science above all sciences, which deals with the foundation of the Universe, with the constitution of matter from which everything in the Universe is made, and with the ether of space by which alone the various portions of matter forming the Universe affect each other even at such distances as we may never expect to traverse whatever the progress of our science in the future.

We, who have devoted our lives to the solution of problems connected with physics, now meet together to help each other and to forward the interests of the subject which we love. A subject which appeals most strongly to the better instincts of our nature, and the problems of which tax our minds to the limit of their capacity and suggest the grandest and noblest ideas of which they are capable.

In a country where the doctrine of the equal rights of man has been distorted to mean the equality of man in other respects, we form a small and unique body of men, a new variety of the human race, as one of our greatest scientists calls it, whose views of what constitutes the greatest achievement in life are very different from those around us. In this respect we form an aristocracy, not of wealth, not of pedigree, but of intellect and of ideals, holding him in the highest respect who adds the most to our knowledge or who strives after it as the highest good.

Thus we meet together for mutual sympathy and the interchange of knowledge, and may we do so ever with appreciation of the benefits to ourselves and possibly to our science. Above all, let us cultivate the idea of the dignity of our pursuit, so that this feeling may sustain us in the midst of a world which gives its highest praise, not to the investigation in the pure etherial physics which our society is formed to cultivate, but to the one who uses it for satisfying the physical rather than the intellectual needs of mankind. He who makes two blades of grass grow where one grew before is the benefactor of mankind; but he who obscurely worked to find the laws of such growth is the intellectual superior as well as the greater benefactor of the two.

How stands our country, then, in this respect? My answer must still be now as it was fifteen years ago, that much of the intellect of the country is still wasted in the pursuit of so-called practical science which ministers to our physical needs and but little thought and money is given to the grander portion of the subject which appeals to our intellect alone. But your presence here gives evidence that such a condition is not to last forever.

Even in the past we have the names of a few whom scientists throughout the world delight to honor. Franklin, who almost revolutionized the science of electricity by a few simple but profound experiments. Count Rumford, whose experiments almost demonstrated the nature of heat. Henry, who might have done much for the progress of physics had he published more fully the results of his investigations. Mayer, whose simple and ingenious experiments have been a source of pleasure and profit to many. This is the meager list of those whom death allows me to speak of and who have earned mention here by doing something for the progress of our science. And yet the record has been searched for more than a hundred years. How different had I started to record those who have made useful and beneficial inventions!

But I know, when I look in the faces of those before me, where the eager intellect and high purpose sit enthroned on bodies possessing the vigor and strength of youth, that the writer of a hundred years hence can no longer throw such a reproach upon our country. Nor can we blame those who have gone before us. The progress of every science shows us the condition of its growth. Very few persons, if isolated in a semi-civilized land, have either the desire or the opportunity of pursuing the higher branches of science. Even if they should be able to do so, their influence on their science depends upon what they publish and make known to the world. A hermit philosopher we can imagine might make many useful discoveries. Yet, if he keeps them to himself, he can never claim to have benefited the world in any degree. His unpublished results are his private gain, but the world is no better off until he has made them known in language strong enough to call attention to them and to convince the world of their truth. Thus, to encourage the growth of any science, the best thing we can do is to meet together in its interest, to discuss its problems, to criticise each other's work and, best of all, to provide means by which the better portion of it may be made known to the world. Furthermore, let us encourage discrimination in our thoughts and work. Let us recognize the eras when great thoughts have been introduced into our subject and let us honor the great men who introduced and proved them correct. Let us forever reject such foolish ideas as the equality of mankind and carefully give the greater credit to the greater man. So, in choosing the subjects for our investigation, let us, if possible, work upon those subjects which will finally give us an advanced knowledge of some great subject. I am aware that we cannot always do this : our ideas will often flow in side channels : but, with the great problems of the Universe before us, we may sometime be able to do our share toward the greater end.

What is matter ; what is gravitation ; what is ether and the radiation through it ; what is electricity and magnetism ; how are these connected together and what is their relation to heat ? These are the greater problems of the universe But many infinitely smaller problems we must attack and solve before we can even guess at the solution of the greater ones.

In our attitude toward these greater problems how do we stand and what is the foundation of our knowledge ?

Newton and the great array of astronomers who have succeeded him have proved that, within planetary distances, matter attracts all others with a force varying inversely as the square of the distance. But what sort of proof have we of this law ? It is derived from astronomical observations on the planetary orbits. It agrees very well within these immense spaces ; but where is the evidence that the law holds for smaller distances ? We measure the lunar distance and the size of the earth and compare the force at that dis-

HENRY AUGUSTUS ROWLAND

tance with the force of gravitation on the earth's surface.   But to do this we must compare the matter in the earth with that in the sun.   This we can only do by *assuming* the law to be proved. Again, in descending from the earth's gravitation to that of two small bodies, as in the Cavendish experiment, we *assume* the law to hold and deduce the mass of the earth in terms of our unit of mass. Hence, when we say that the mass of the earth is 5½ times that of an equal volume of water we *assume* the law of gravitation to be that of Newton.   Thus a proof of the law from planetary down to terrestrial distances is physically impossible.

Again, that portion of the law which says that gravitational attraction is proportional to the quantity of matter, which is the same as saying that the attraction of one body by another is not affected by the presence of a third, the feeble proof that we give by weighing bodies in a balance in different positions with respect to each other cannot be accepted on a larger scale.   When we can tear the sun into two portions and prove that either of the two halves attracts half as much as the whole, then we shall have a proof worth mentioning.

Then as to the relation of gravitation and time what can we say ? Can we for a moment suppose that two bodies moving through space with great velocities have their gravitation unaltered ?   I think not.   Neither can we accept Laplace's proof that the force of gravitation acts instantaneously through space, for we can readily imagine some compensating features unthought of by Laplace.

How little we know then of this law which has been under observation for two hundred years !

Then as to matter itself how have our views changed and how are they constantly changing.   The round hard atom of Newton which God alone could break into pieces has become a molecule composed of many atoms, and each of these smaller atoms has become so elastic that after vibrating 100,000 times its amplitude of vibration is scarcely diminished.   It has become so complicated that it can vibrate with as many thousand notes.   We cover the atom with patches of electricity here and there and make of it a system compared with which the planetary system, nay the universe itself, is simplicity.   Nay more : some of us even claim the power, which Newton attributed to God alone, of breaking the atom into smaller pieces whose size is left to the imagination. Where, then, is that person who ignorantly sneers at the study of matter as a material and gross study? Where, again, is that man with gifts so God-like and mind so elevated that he can attack and solve its problem?

To all matter we attribute two properties, gravitation and inertia. Without these two matter cannot exist. The greatest of the natural laws states that the power of gravitational attraction is proportional to the mass of the body. This law of Newton, almost neglected in the thoughts of physicists, undoubtedly has vast import of the very deepest meaning. Shall it mean that all matter is finally constructed of uniform and similar primordial atoms, or can we find some other explanation?

That the molecules of matter are not round, we know from the facts of crystallography and the action of matter in rotating the plane of polarization of light.

That portions of the molecules and even of the atoms are electrically charged, we know from electrolysis, the action of gases in a vacuum tube, and from the Zeeman effect.

That some of them act like little magnets, we know from the magnetic action of iron, nickel, and cobalt.

That they are elastic the spectrum shows, and that the vibrating portion carries the electric charge with it is shown by the Zeeman effect.

Here, then, we have made quite a start in our problem: but how far are we from the complete solution? How can we imagine the material of which ordinary or primordial atoms are made, dealing as we do only with aggregations of atoms alone? Forever beyond our sight, vibrating an almost infinite number of times in a second, moving hither and yon with restless energy at all temperatures beyond the absolute zero of temperature, it is certainly a wonderful feat of human reason and imagination that we know as much as we do at present. Encouraged by these results, let us not linger too long in their contemplation but press forward to the new discoveries which await us in the future.

Then as to electricity, the subtle spirit of the amber, the demon who reached out his gluttonous arms to draw in the light bodies within his reach, the fluid which could run through metals with the greatest ease but could be stopped by a frail piece of glass! Where

HENRY AUGUSTUS ROWLAND

is it now ? Vanished, thrown on the waste heap of our discarded theories, to be replaced by a far nobler and exalted one of action in the ether of space.

And so we are brought to consider that other great entity—the ether : filling all space without limit, we imagine the ether to be the only means by which two portions of matter distant from each other can have any mutual action. By its means we imagine every atom in the universe to be bound to every other atom by the force of gravitation and often by the force of magnetic and electric action, and we conceive that it alone conveys the vibratory motion of each atom or molecule out into space to be ever lost in endless radiation, passing out into infinite space or absorbed by some other atoms which happen to be in its path. By it all electromagnetic energy is conveyed, from the feeble attraction of the rubbed amber, through the many thousand horse-power conveyed by the electric wires from Niagara, to the mighty rush of energy always flowing from the Sun in a flood of radiation. Actions feeble and actions mighty, from inter-molecular distances through inter-planetary and inter-stellar dis-tances until we reach the mighty distances which bound the Uni-verse—all have their being in this wonderous ether.

And yet, however wonderful it may be, its laws are far more simple than those of matter. Every wave in it, whatever its length or intensity, proceeds onwards in it according to well known laws, all with the same speed, unaltered in direction, from its source in electrified matter to the confines of the Universe, unimpaired in energy unless it is disturbed by the presence of matter. However the waves may cross each other, each proceeds by itself without interference with the others.

So with regard to gravitation, we have no evidence that the presence of a third body affects the mutual attraction of two other bodies, or that the presence of a third quantity of electricity affects the mutual attraction of two other quantities. The same for magnetism.

For this reason the laws of gravitation and of electric and mag-netic action including radiation are the simplest of all laws when we confine them to a so-called vacuum, but become more and more complicated when we treat of them in space containing matter.

Subject the ether to immense electrostatic magnetic or gravitational forces and we find absolutely no signs of its breaking down or even a change in its properties.   Set it into vibration by means of an intensely hot body like that of the sun and it conveys many thousand horse-power for each square foot of surface as quietly and with apparently as unchanged laws as if it were conveying the energy of a tallow dip.

Again, subject a millimeter of ether to the stress of many thousand, nay even a million, volts and yet we see no signs of breaking down.

Hence the properties of the ether are of ideal simplicity and lead to the simplest of natural laws.   All forces which act at a distance always obey the law of the inverse square of the distance and we have also the attraction of any number of parts placed near each other equal to the arithmetical sum of the attractions when those parts are separated.   So also the simple law of etherial waves which has been mentioned above.

At the present time, through the labors of Maxwell supplemented by those of Hertz and others, we have arrived at the great generalization that all wave disturbances in the ether are electromagnetic in their nature.   We know of little or no etherial disturbance which can be set up by the motion of matter alone : the matter must be electrified in order to have sufficient hold on the ether to communicate its motion to the ether.   The Zeeman effect even shows this to be the case where molecules are concerned and when the period of vibration is immensely great.   Indeed the experiment on the magnetic action of electric convection shows the same thing.   By electrifying a disc in motion it appears as if the disc holds fast to the ether and drags it with it, thus setting up the peculiar etherial motion known as magnetism.

Have we not another case of a similar nature when a huge gravitational mass like that of the earth revolves on its axis?   Has not matter a feeble hold on the ether sufficient to produce the earth's magnetism ?

But the experiment of Lodge to detect such an action apparently showed that it must be very feeble.   Might not his experiment have succeeded had he used an electrified revolving disc ?

To detect something dependent on the relative motion of the ether and matter has been and is the great desire of physicists. But we always find that, with one possible exception, there is always

97

HENRY AUGUSTUS ROWLAND

some compensating feature which renders our efforts useless. This one experiment is the aberration of light, but even here Stokes has shown that it may be explained in either of two ways : first, that the earth moves through the ether of space without disturbing it, and second, if it carries the ether with it by a kind of motion called irrotational. Even here, however, the amount of action probably depends upon *relative* motion of the luminous source to the recipient telescope.

So the principle of Doppler depends also on this relative motion and is independent of the ether.

The result of the experiments of Foucault on the passage of light through moving water can no longer be interpreted as due to the partial movement of the ether with the moving water, an inference due to imperfect theory alone. The experiment of Lodge, who attempted to set the ether in motion by a rapidly rotating disc, showed no such result.

The experiment of Michelson to detect the etherial wind, although carried to the extreme of accuracy, also failed to detect any relative motion of the matter and the ether.

But matter with an electrical charge holds fast to the ether and moves it in the manner required for magnetic action,

When electrified bodies move together through space or with reference to each other we can only follow their mutual actions through very slow and uniform velocities. When they move with velocities comparable with that of light, equal to it or even beyond it, we calculate their mutual actions or action on the ether only by the light of our imagination unguided by experiment. The conclusions of J. J. Thomson, Heaviside, and Hertz are all results of the imagination and they all rest upon assumptions more or less reasonable but always assumptions. A mathematical investigation always obeys the law of the conservation of knowledge : we never get out more from it than we put in. The knowledge may be changed in form, it may be clearer and more exactly stated, but the total amount of the knowledge of nature given out by the investigation is the same as we started with. Hence we can never predict the result in the case of velocities beyond our reach, and such calculations as the velocity of the cathode rays from their electromagnetic action has a great element of uncertainty which we should do well to remember.

Indeed, when it comes to exact knowledge, the limits are far more circumscribed.

How is it, then, that we hear physicists and others constantly stating what will happen beyond these limits? Take velocities, for instance, such as that of a material body moving with the velocity of light. There is no known process by which such a velocity can be obtained even though the body fell from an infinite distance upon the largest aggregation of matter in the Universe. If we electrify it, as in the cathode rays, its properties are so changed that the matter properties are completely masked by the electromagnetic.

It is a common error which young physicists are apt to fall into to obtain a law, a curve, or a mathematical expression for given experimental limits and then to apply it to points outside those limits. This is sometimes called extrapolation. Such a process, unless carefully guarded, ceases to be a reasoning process and becomes one of pure imagination specially liable to error when the distance is too great.

But it is not my purpose to enter into detail. What I have given suffices to show how little we know of the profounder questions involved in our subject.

It is a curious fact that, having minds tending to the infinite, with imaginations unlimited by time and space, the limits of our exact knowledge are very small indeed. In time we are limited by a few hundred or possibly thousand years : indeed the limit in our science is far less than the smaller of these periods. In space we have exact knowledge limited to portions of our earth's surface and a mile or so below the surface, together with what little we can learn from looking through powerful telescopes into the space beyond. In temperature our knowledge extends from near the absolute zero to that of the sun, but exact knowledge is far more limited. In pressures we go from the Crookse vacuum still containing myriads of flying atoms to pressures limited by the strength of steel, but still very minute compared with the pressure at the center of the earth and sun, where the hardest steel would flow like the most limpid water. In velocities we are limited to a few miles per second.

99

HENRY AUGUSTUS ROWLAND

In forces to possibly 100 tons to the square inch. In mechanical rotations to a few hundred times per second.

All the facts which we have considered, the liability to error in whatever direction we go, the infirmity of our minds in their reasoning power, the fallibility of witnesses and experimenters, lead the scientist to be specially skeptical with reference to any statement made to him or any so-called knowledge which may be brought to his attention. The facts and theories of our science are so much more certain than those of history, of the testimony of ordinary people on which the facts of ordinary history or of legal evidence rest, or of the value of medicines to which we trust when we are ill, indeed to the whole fabric of supposed truth by which an ordinary person guides his belief and the actions of his life, that it may seem ominous and strange if what I have said of the imperfections of the knowledge of physics is correct. How shall we regulate our mind with respect to it : there is only one way that I know of and that is to avoid the discontinuity of the ordinary, indeed the so-called cultivated legal mind. There is no such thing as absolute truth and absolute falsehood. The scientific mind should never recognize the perfect truth or the perfect falsehood of any supposed theory or observation. It should carefully weigh the chances of truth and error and grade each in its proper position along the line joining absolute truth and absolute error.

The ordinary crude mind has only two compartments, one for truth and one for error ; indeed the contents of the two compartments are sadly mixed in most cases ; the ideal scientific mind, however, has an infinite number. Each theory or law is in its proper compartment indicating the probability of its truth. As a new fact arrives the scientist changes it from one compartment to another so as, if possible, to always keep it in its proper relation to truth and error. Thus the fluid nature of electricity was once in a compartment near the truth. Faraday's and Maxwell's researches have now caused us to move it to a compartment nearly up to that of absolute error.

So the law of gravitation within planetary distances is far toward absolute truth, but may still need amending before it is advanced farther in that direction.

The ideal scientific mind, therefore, must always be held in a state of balance which the slightest new evidence may change in one direction or another. It is in a constant state of skepticism, knowing full well that nothing is certain. It is above all an agnostic with respect to all facts and theories of science as well as to all other so-called beliefs and theories.

Yet it would be folly to reason from this that we need not guide our life according to the approach to knowledge that we possess. Nature is inexorable ; it punishes the child who unknowingly steps off a precipice quite as severely as the grown scientist who steps over, with full knowledge of all the laws of falling bodies and the chances of their being correct. Both fall to the bottom and in their fall obey the gravitational laws of inorganic matter, slightly modified by the muscular contortions of the falling object, but not in any degree changed by the previous belief of the person. Natural laws there probably are, rigid and unchanging ones at that. Understand them and they are beneficent : we can use them for our purposes and make them the slaves of our desires. Misunderstand them and they are monsters who may grind us to powder or crush us in the dust. Nothing is asked of us as to our belief : they act unswervingly and we must understand them or suffer the consequences. Our only course, then, is to act according to the chances of our knowing the right laws. If we act correctly, right ; if we act incorrectly, we suffer. If we are ignorant we die. What greater fool, then, than he who states that belief is of no consequence provided it is sincere.

An only child, a beloved wife, lies on a bed of illness. The physician says that the disease is mortal ; a minute plant called a microbe has obtained entrance into the body and is growing at the expense of its tissues, forming deadly poisons in the blood or destroying some vital organ. The physician looks on without being able to do anything. Daily he comes and notes the failing strength of his patient and daily the patient goes downward until he rests in his grave. But why has the physician allowed this ? Can we doubt that there is a remedy which shall kill the microbe or neutralize its poison ? Why, then, has he not used it ? He is employed to cure but has failed. His bill we cheerfully pay because he has done his best and given a chance of cure. The answer is *ignorance*. The remedy is yet unknown. The physician is waiting for others to discover it or perhaps is experimenting in a crude and unscientific manner to find it. Is not the inference correct, then, that the world has been paying the wrong class of men? Would not this ignorance have been dispelled had the proper money been used in the past to dispel it? Such deaths some people consider an act of God. What blasphemy to attribute to God that which is due to our own and our ancestors' selfishness in not founding institutions for medical research in sufficient number and with sufficient means to discover the truth. Such deaths are murder. Thus the present generation suffers for the sins of the past and we die because our ancestors dissipated their wealth in armies and navies, in the foolish pomp and circumstance of society, and neglected to provide us with a knowledge of natural laws. In this sense they were the murderers and robbers of future generations of unborn millions, and have made the world a charnel house and place of mourning where peace and happiness might have been. Only their ignorance of what they were doing can be their excuse, but this excuse puts them in the class of boors and savages who act according to selfish desire and not to reason and to the calls of duty. Let the present generation take warning that this reproach be not cast on it, for it cannot plead ignorance in this respect.

This illustration from the department of medicine I have given because it appeals to all. But all the sciences are linked together and must advance in concert. The human body is a chemical and physical problem, and these sciences must advance before we can conquer disease.

But the true lover of physics needs no such spur to his actions. The cure of disease is a very important object and nothing can be nobler than a life devoted to its cure.

The aims of the physicist, however, are in part purely intellectual : he strives to understand the Universe on account of the intellectual pleasure derived from the pursuit, but he is upheld in it by the knowledge that the study of nature's secrets is the ordained method by which the greatest good and happiness shall finally come to the human race.

Where, then, are the great laboratories of research in this city, in this country, nay, in the world? We see a few miserble structures here and there occupied by a few starving professors who are nobly striving to do the best with the feeble means at their disposal. But where in the world is the institute of pure research in any department of science with an income of $100,000,000 per year. Where can the discoverer in pure science earn more than the wages of a day laborer or cook? But $100,000,000 per year is but the price of an army or of a navy designed to kill other people. Just think of it, that one per cent of this sum seems to most people too great to save our children and descendants from misery and even death!

But the twentieth century is near—may we not hope for better things before its end? May we not hope to influence the public in this direction?

Let us go forward, then, with confidence in the dignity of our pursuit. Let us hold our heads high with a pure conscience while we seek the truth, and may the American Physical Society do its share now and in generations yet to come in trying to unravel the great problem of the constitution and laws of the Universe.

103

HENRY AUGUSTUS ROWLAND

JOSIAH
WILLARD
GIBBS

1839-1903

In 1900 there were at most a thousand physicists in the world. About one-fourth of these were in the United States, more than in any other single country; American physics had finally come to the level prevailing in the old European nations. Nevertheless American physicists were not making great discoveries as often as their numbers would suggest. This was partly because many of them were in colleges where research was still only tolerated rather than encouraged, and partly because Americans were notoriously weak in theoretical physics.

The case of Willard Gibbs shows that this weakness was due to tradition and training, not to any lack of native talent. Gibbs, son of a Yale professor of sacred literature, descended from a long line of New England college graduates. He studied at Yale, received his Ph.D. there in 1863—one of the first doctorates granted in the United States—tutored Latin and natural philosophy there, and then left for three decisive years in Europe. Up to that time Gibbs had shown interest in both mathematics and engineering, which he combined in his dissertation "On the Form of the Teeth of Wheels in Spur Gearing." The lectures he attended in Paris, Berlin and Heidelberg, given by some of the greatest men of the day, changed him once and for all. In 1871, two years after his return from Europe, he became Yale's first Professor of Mathematical Physics. He had not yet published any papers on this subject. For nine years he held the position without pay, living on the comfortable inheritance his father had left; only when Johns Hopkins University offered Gibbs a post did Yale give him a small salary.

Gibbs never married. He lived out a calm and uneventful life in the house where he grew up, which he shared with his sisters. He was a gentle and considerate man, well-liked by those who knew him, but he tended to avoid society and was little known even in

New Haven. Nor was he known to more than a few of the world's scientists—partly because his writings were extremely compact, abstract and difficult. As one of Gibbs' European colleagues wrote, "Having once condensed a truth into a concise and very general formula, he would not think of churning out the endless succession of specific cases that were implied by the general proposition; his intelligence, like his character, was of a retiring disposition." The Europeans paid for their failure to read Gibbs: A large part of the work they did in thermodynamics before the turn of the century could have been found already in his published work.

Gibbs' chief scientific papers appeared in the *Transactions* of the Connecticut Academy of Arts and Sciences. The articles were expensive to set in type because of their length and their wealth of mathematical formulas, so funds were raised by subscription from Yale professors and New Haven businessmen, few or none of whom could understand the publication they were subsidizing. The Connecticut Academy's *Transactions* were little read, but Gibbs tried to make his results known by mailing many reprints and by publishing a summary elsewhere.

In these papers Gibbs' starting point for analyzing a system was the state of equilibrium, which (as he pointed out) is characterized by a maximum in the system's entropy. This principle, he noted, was already known to physicists, but "its importance does not appear to have been appreciated. Little has been done to develop the principle as a foundation for the general theory of thermodynamic equilibrium." He proceeded to correct this situation, demonstrating for the first time the uses of the differential relationship in a system between energy U, pressure P, volume V, temperature T, and the entropy S, the last a quantity then scarcely understood: $dU = TdS - PdV$. Adding terms to allow for variations in the chemical constitution of the system, he derived an astonishing variety of consequences. Many phenomena which had never been within the domain of thermodynamics were now annexed by this equation, including elastic and surface phenomena, changes of phase, and a great part of chemistry.

Once this was completed Gibbs turned to another subject. In 1892 he wrote Lord Rayleigh with characteristic modesty, "Just now I am trying to get ready for publication something on thermodynamics from the *a priori* point of view, or rather on 'Statistical Mechanics'. . . I do not know that I shall have anything particularly new in substance, but shall be contented if I can so choose my standpoint (as seems to me possible) as to get a simpler view of the subject." Ten years later this work resulted in a classic book which put statistical mechanics on a new and more general basis.

By the turn of the century Gibbs was becoming fairly well known, as much for his vigorous and partisan defense of the form of vector notation which is now standard as for his more basic work. But aside from summers spent hiking in the mountains, he continued to the end of his days to spend nearly all his time in work or in walking about the few blocks that included his home and his college.

We give here the preface to his book on statistical mechanics, in which he shows something of his aims and methods. Note (p. ix-x) that Gibbs was fully aware of the problems that were to lead to quantum mechanics. Note too that it is not until the last chapter of the book that Gibbs restricts himself to anything so lacking in generality as a system composed of molecules.

ELEMENTARY PRINCIPLES

IN

STATISTICAL MECHANICS

DEVELOPED WITH ESPECIAL REFERENCE TO

THE RATIONAL FOUNDATION OF THERMODYNAMICS

BY

J. WILLARD GIBBS

Professor of Mathematical Physics in Yale University

NEW YORK: CHARLES SCRIBNER'S SONS
LONDON: EDWARD ARNOLD
1902

PREFACE.

THE usual point of view in the study of mechanics is that where the attention is mainly directed to the changes which take place in the course of time in a given system. The principal problem is the determination of the condition of the system with respect to configuration and velocities at any required time, when its condition in these respects has been given for some one time, and the fundamental equations are those which express the changes continually taking place in the system. Inquiries of this kind are often simplified by taking into consideration conditions of the system other than those through which it actually passes or is supposed to pass, but our attention is not usually carried beyond conditions differing infinitesimally from those which are regarded as actual.

For some purposes, however, it is desirable to take a broader view of the subject. We may imagine a great number of systems of the same nature, but differing in the configurations and velocities which they have at a given instant, and differing not merely infinitesimally, but it may be so as to embrace every conceivable combination of configuration and velocities. And here we may set the problem, not to follow a particular system through its succession of configurations, but to determine how the whole number of systems will be distributed among the various conceivable configurations and velocities at any required time, when the distribution has been given for some one time. The fundamental equation for this inquiry is that which gives the rate of change of the number of systems which fall within any infinitesimal limits of configuration and velocity.

JOSIAH WILLARD GIBBS

Such inquiries have been called by Maxwell *statistical.* They belong to a branch of mechanics which owes its origin to the desire to explain the laws of thermodynamics on mechanical principles, and of which Clausius, Maxwell, and Boltzmann are to be regarded as the principal founders. The first inquiries in this field were indeed somewhat narrower in their scope than that which has been mentioned, being applied to the particles of a system, rather than to independent systems. Statistical inquiries were next directed to the phases (or conditions with respect to configuration and velocity) which succeed one another in a given system in the course of time. The explicit consideration of a great number of systems and their distribution in phase, and of the permanence or alteration of this distribution in the course of time is perhaps first found in Boltzmann's paper on the " Zusammenhang zwischen den Sätzen über das Verhalten mehratomiger Gasmoleküle mit Jacobi's Princip des letzten Multiplicators " (1871).

But although, as a matter of history, statistical mechanics owes its origin to investigations in thermodynamics, it seems eminently worthy of an independent development, both on account of the elegance and simplicity of its principles, and because it yields new results and places old truths in a new light in departments quite outside of thermodynamics. Moreover, the separate study of this branch of mechanics seems to afford the best foundation for the study of rational thermodynamics and molecular mechanics.

The laws of thermodynamics, as empirically determined, express the approximate and probable behavior of systems of a great number of particles, or, more precisely, they express the laws of mechanics for such systems as they appear to beings who have not the fineness of perception to enable them to appreciate quantities of the order of magnitude of those which relate to single particles, and who cannot repeat their experiments often enough to obtain any but the most probable results. The laws of statistical mechanics apply to conservative systems of any number of degrees of freedom,

110

JOSIAH WILLARD GIBBS

and are exact. This does not make them more difficult to establish than the approximate laws for systems of a great many degrees of freedom, or for limited classes of such systems. The reverse is rather the case, for our attention is not diverted from what is essential by the peculiarities of the system considered, and we are not obliged to satisfy ourselves that the effect of the quantities and circumstances neglected will be negligible in the result. The laws of thermodynamics may be easily obtained from the principles of statistical mechanics, of which they are the incomplete expression, but they make a somewhat blind guide in our search for those laws. This is perhaps the principal cause of the slow progress of rational thermodynamics, as contrasted with the rapid deduction of the consequences of its laws as empirically established. To this must be added that the rational foundation of thermodynamics lay in a branch of mechanics of which the fundamental notions and principles, and the characteristic operations, were alike unfamiliar to students of mechanics.

We may therefore confidently believe that nothing will more conduce to the clear apprehension of the relation of thermodynamics to rational mechanics, and to the interpretation of observed phenomena with reference to their evidence respecting the molecular constitution of bodies, than the study of the fundamental notions and principles of that department of mechanics to which thermodynamics is especially related.

Moreover, we avoid the gravest difficulties when, giving up the attempt to frame hypotheses concerning the constitution of material bodies, we pursue statistical inquiries as a branch of rational mechanics. In the present state of science, it seems hardly possible to frame a dynamic theory of molecular action which shall embrace the phenomena of thermodynamics, of radiation, and of the electrical manifestations which accompany the union of atoms. Yet any theory is obviously inadequate which does not take account of all these phenomena. Even if we confine our attention to the

111

JOSIAH WILLARD GIBBS

phenomena distinctively thermodynamic, we do not escape difficulties in as simple a matter as the number of degrees of freedom of a diatomic gas. It is well known that while theory would assign to the gas six degrees of freedom per molecule, in our experiments on specific heat we cannot account for more than five. Certainly, one is building on an insecure foundation, who rests his work on hypotheses concerning the constitution of matter.

Difficulties of this kind have deterred the author from attempting to explain the mysteries of nature, and have forced him to be contented with the more modest aim of deducing some of the more obvious propositions relating to the statistical branch of mechanics. Here, there can be no mistake in regard to the agreement of the hypotheses with the facts of nature, for nothing is assumed in that respect. The only error into which one can fall, is the want of agreement between the premises and the conclusions, and this, with care, one may hope, in the main, to avoid.

The matter of the present volume consists in large measure of results which have been obtained by the investigators mentioned above, although the point of view and the arrangement may be different. These results, given to the public one by one in the order of their discovery, have necessarily, in their original presentation, not been arranged in the most logical manner.

In the first chapter we consider the general problem which has been mentioned, and find what may be called the fundamental equation of statistical mechanics. A particular case of this equation will give the condition of statistical equilibrium, *i. e.*, the condition which the distribution of the systems in phase must satisfy in order that the distribution shall be permanent. In the general case, the fundamental equation admits an integration, which gives a principle which may be variously expressed, according to the point of view from which it is regarded, as the conservation of density-in-phase, or of extension-in-phase, or of probability of phase.

In the second chapter, we apply this principle of conservation of probability of phase to the theory of errors in the calculated phases of a system, when the determination of the arbitrary constants of the integral equations are subject to error. In this application, we do not go beyond the usual approximations. In other words, we combine the principle of conservation of probability of phase, which is exact, with those approximate relations, which it is customary to assume in the " theory of errors."

In the third chapter we apply the principle of conservation of extension-in-phase to the integration of the differential equations of motion. This gives Jacobi's "last multiplier," as has been shown by Boltzmann.

In the fourth and following chapters we return to the consideration of statistical equilibrium, and confine our attention to conservative systems. We consider especially ensembles of systems in which the index (or logarithm) of probability of phase is a linear function of the energy. This distribution, on account of its unique importance in the theory of statistical equilibrium, I have ventured to call *canonical*, and the divisor of the energy, the *modulus* of distribution. The moduli of ensembles have properties analogous to temperature, in that equality of the moduli is a condition of equilibrium with respect to exchange of energy, when such exchange is made possible.

We find a differential equation relating to average values in the ensemble which is identical in form with the fundamental differential equation of thermodynamics, the average index of probability of phase, with change of sign, corresponding to entropy, and the modulus to temperature.

For the average square of the anomalies of the energy, we find an expression which vanishes in comparison with the square of the average energy, when the number of degrees of freedom is indefinitely increased. An ensemble of systems in which the number of degrees of freedom is of the same order of magnitude as the number of molecules in the bodies with which we experiment, if distributed canonically, would therefore appear to human observation as an ensemble of systems in which all have the same energy.

We meet with other quantities, in the development of the subject, which, when the number of degrees of freedom is very great, coincide sensibly with the modulus, and with the average index of probability, taken negatively, in a canonical ensemble, and which, therefore, may also be regarded as corresponding to temperature and entropy. The correspondence is however imperfect, when the number of degrees of freedom is not very great, and there is nothing to recommend these quantities except that in definition they may be regarded as more simple than those which have been mentioned. In Chapter XIV, this subject of thermodynamic analogies is discussed somewhat at length.

Finally, in Chapter XV, we consider the modification of the preceding results which is necessary when we consider systems composed of a number of entirely similar particles, or, it may be, of a number of particles of several kinds, all of each kind being entirely similar to each other, and when one of the variations to be considered is that of the numbers of the particles of the various kinds which are contained in a system. This supposition would naturally have been introduced earlier, if our object had been simply the expression of the laws of nature. It seemed desirable, however, to separate sharply the purely thermodynamic laws from those special modifications which belong rather to the theory of the properties of matter.

J. W. G.

New Haven, December, 1901.

ROBERT ANDREWS MILLIKAN

1868-1953

During Robert A. Millikan's lifetime the number of physicists in the United States doubled about every ten years, and the laboratory space and research funds at their disposal grew even faster. Millikan benefited from this trend and worked vigorously to accelerate it. He was of native American stock, raised in the large and cheerful family of an Iowa preacher. At Oberlin College he taught himself the elements of physics, for nobody there knew enough to teach him. Robust and athletic, he considered making a career in physical education until one of his professors persuaded him to go to Columbia University; there his real education began. He next studied in Germany, as was the custom for young American scientists of his generation—during his summer in Göttingen he found more Americans than Germans among the advanced students in the laboratory. While he was there he got a message from A. A. Michelson, offering him a teaching assistantship at Chicago. Millikan jumped at it, although he could have had an appointment elsewhere at twice the salary, for Michelson promised that he could spend up to half his time doing his own research, a privilege not granted at most colleges. At Chicago Millikan began work in various areas such as electrical discharges.

But it was as a teacher and textbook writer that Millikan first made his mark. In collaboration he wrote elementary texts that educated a generation of Americans, and in the classroom he proved to be an outstanding educator. These qualities were valued at Chicago, but not as much as research. Millikan was appointed associate professor only at the age of 38, in a time when the median American physicist became a *full* professor at the age of 32. He later recalled: "Although I had for ten years spent on research every hour I could spare from my other pressing duties, by 1906 I knew that I had not yet published results of outstanding importance, and certainly had not attained a position of much distinction as a research physicist." He thought of devoting himself wholly to education. But instead he stopped writing textbooks and set out on one last try at a new line of research: the determination of the elementary unit of electric charge.

The Millikan oil-drop experiment was far superior to previous determinations of the charge of an electron. Where other workers had attempted to measure the quantity by observing the effect of an electric field on a cloud of water droplets, Millikan used single drops, first of water and then, when he found these evaporating, of oil. His measurement was off by only 0.5%, and most of this error was due to his adoption of a plausible but wrong value for the viscosity of air. The experiment had broader significance than a simple refinement of a number. Millikan emphasized that the very nature of his data refuted conclusively the minority of scientists who still held that electrons (and perhaps atoms too) were not necessarily fundamental, discrete particles. And he provided a value for the electronic charge which, when inserted in Niels Bohr's theoretical formula for the hydrogen spectrum, accurately gave the Rydberg constant—the first and most convincing proof of Bohr's quantum theory of the atom.

Shortly after the experiment's publication in 1910, Millikan was rewarded with a full professorship. His next set of experiments, on the photo-electric effect, was equally fruitful; by 1915 he had proved that Einstein's formula for this effect was correct—which was against his own expectations.

Early in 1917 Millikan went to Washington to be executive officer of the National Research Council of the National Academy of Sciences, charged with war research on the detection of submarines and other essential problems. This work threw him into contact with the astrophysicist George Ellery Hale, one of America's chief organizers of science. After the war Hale bombarded Millikan with requests to join him at the new and still obscure California Institute of Technology. Since physics was to be the centerpiece of the Institute and since Millikan was promised lavish funds and a free hand, in 1921 he agreed to come. Under his guidance Caltech almost immediately entered the top rank of American research centers. Convinced by his wartime experience that physics must be organized and funded for the benefit of the nation, Millikan soon became well-known to the public as a vigorous spokesman for science and education and a busy money-raiser; he was also a promoter of the reconciliation of science with religion.

His fame was enhanced by continuing scientific work — above all his studies of the phenomenon he named "cosmic rays". He stubbornly insisted that these rays consisted in whole or in large part of electromagnetic radiation, but this error did not prevent him from performing or inspiring much work of basic importance. With his collaborator Ira Bowen he meanwhile opened up the field of vacuum ultraviolet spectroscopy. At the same time he continued his outstanding contributions to education, helping administer Caltech and personally attracting and inspiring a constant stream of students.

We excerpt here Millikan's final report on his early oil drop experiments, taken from the *Physical Review* (ser. 2, vol. 2, 1913, p. 109-43). This journal was founded at Cornell in 1893, taken over by The American Physical Society in 1913, and grew swiftly until it became the most-cited physics journal in the world, a mark it passed around 1930. In Millikan's day journals received far fewer papers and did not have to severely restrict their length, so we may witness in detail the ingenuity, thoroughness and logic needed for such landmark work.

THE

PHYSICAL REVIEW

A Journal of Experimental and Theoretical Physics

CONDUCTED BY

THE

American Physical Society

Vol. II., Series II.

THE PHYSICAL REVIEW

LANCASTER, PA., AND ITHACA, N. Y.

1913

119

ROBERT ANDREWS MILLIKAN

ON THE ELEMENTARY ELECTRICAL CHARGE AND THE AVOGADRO CONSTANT.

By R. A. Millikan.

1. Introductory.

THE experiments herewith reported were undertaken with the view of introducing certain improvements into the oil-drop method[1] of determining e and N and thus obtaining a higher accuracy than had before been possible in the evaluation of these most fundamental constants.

In the original observations by this method such excellent agreement was found between the values of e derived from different measurements (l. c., p. 384) that it was evident that if appreciable errors existed they must be looked for in the constant factors entering into the final formula rather than in inaccuracies in the readings or irregularities in the behavior of the drops. Accordingly a systematic redetermination of all these constants was begun some three years ago. The relative importance of the various factors may be seen from the following review.

As is now well known the oil-drop method rested originally upon the assumption of Stokes's law and gave the charge e on a given drop through the equation

$$e_n = \frac{4}{3} \pi \left(\frac{9\eta}{2} \right)^{\frac{3}{2}} \left(\frac{1}{g(\sigma - \rho)} \right)^{\frac{1}{2}} \frac{(v_1 + v_2)v_1^{\frac{1}{2}}}{F}, \tag{1}$$

in which η is the coefficient of viscosity of air, σ the density of the oil, ρ that of the air, v_1 the speed of descent of the drop under gravity and v_2 its speed of ascent under the influence of an electric field of strength F.

The essential feature of the method consisted in repeatedly changing the charge on a given drop by the capture of ions from the air and in thus obtaining a series of charges with each drop. These charges showed a very exact multiple relationship under all circumstances—a fact which demonstrated very directly the atomic structure of the electric charge. If Stokes's law were correct the greatest common divisor of this series of charges should have been the absolute value of the elementary electrical charge. But the fact that this greatest common divisor failed to come out a constant when drops of different sizes were used showed that Stokes's

---

[1] R. A. Millikan, Phys. Rev., 32, pp. 349–397, 1911.

law breaks down when the diameter of a drop begins to approach the order of magnitude of the mean free path of a gas molecule. Consequently the following corrected form of Stokes's law for the speed of a drop falling under gravity was suggested.

$$v_1 = \frac{2}{9} \frac{ga^2(\sigma - \rho)}{\eta} \left\{ 1 + A\frac{l}{a} \right\}, \tag{2}$$

in which a is the radius of the drop, l the mean free path of a gas molecule and A an undetermined constant. It is to be particularly emphasized that the term in the brackets was expressly set up merely as a first order correction term in l/a *and involved no theoretical assumptions of any sort;* further that *the constant A was empirically determined* through the use only of small values of l/a and that *the values of e and N obtained were therefore precisely as trustworthy as were the observations themselves.* This fact has been repeatedly overlooked in criticisms of the results of the oil-drop method.[1]

Calling then e_1 the greatest common divisor of all the various values of e_n found in a series of observations on a given drop there resulted from the combination of (1) and (2) the equation

$$e\left(1 + A\frac{l}{a} \right)^{\frac{3}{2}} = e_1, \tag{3}$$

or

[1] Indeed M. Jules Roux (Compt. Rendu, 152, p. 1168, May, 1911) has attempted to correct my values of e and N by reducing some observations like mine which he made on droplets of sulphur, with the aid of a purely theoretical value of A which is actually approximately twice too large. The impossibility of the value of A which he assumes he would himself have discovered had he made observations on spheres of different sizes or at different pressures. Such observations whether made on solid spheres or on liquid spheres always yield a value of A about half of that assumed by Roux. Hence his value of e, viz., $e = 4.17 \times 10^{-10}$ rests on no sort of experimental foundation whatsoever. It rests rather on two erroneous assumptions, first the assumption of the correctness of the constants in Cunningham's theoretical equation (Proc. Roy. Soc., 83, p. 357; see also footnote 3, p. 380, Phys. Rev., Vol. 32)—constants which I shall presently show are in no case correct within the limits of experimental error even when inelastic impact is assumed, and second, the assumption that molecules make elastic impact against solid surfaces, an assumption which is completely incorrect as I had already proved by showing that the value of the "slip" term is the same for oil and air as for glass and air (Phys. Rev., Vol. 32, p. 382), which Knudsen also had proved experimentally to be erroneous (Knudsen, An. der Phys., 28, p. 75, 1909, and 35, p. 389) and which for theoretical reasons as well is plainly inadmissible, since were it correct Poiseuille's law could not hold for gases under any circumstances.

But even if Roux had assumed the correct value of A he would still have obtained results several per cent. too low, a fact which must be ascribed either to faulty experimental arrangements or to imperfect knowledge of the density of his sulphur spheres; *for solid spheres have been very carefully studied in the Ryerson Laboratory and are in fact found to yield results very close to those obtained with oil drops.* Solid spheres however are not nearly so well adapted to a precision measurement of e as are oil drops, since their density and sphericity are always matters of some uncertainty.

$$e = \frac{e_1}{\left(1 + A\dfrac{l}{a}\right)^{\frac{2}{3}}}. \tag{4}$$

It was from this equation that e was obtained after A had been found by a graphical method which will be more fully considered presently.

The factors then which enter into the determination of e are: (1) The density factor, $\sigma - \rho$; (2) the electric field strength, F; (3) the viscosity of air, η; (4) the speeds, v_1 and v_2; (5) the drop radius, a; (6) the correction term constant, A.

Concerning the first two of these factors little need be said unless a question be raised as to whether the density of such minute oil drops might not be a function of the radius. Such a question is conclusively answered in the negative both by theory[1] and by the experiments reported in this paper.

Liquid rather than solid spheres were originally chosen because of the far greater certainty with which their density and sphericity could be known. Nevertheless I originally used liquids of widely different viscosities (light oil, glycerine, mercury) and obtained the same results with them all within the limits of error, thus showing experimentally that so far as this work was concerned, the drops all acted like rigid spheres. More complete proof of this conclusion is furnished both by the following observations and by other careful work on solid spheres soon to be reported in detail by Mr. J. Y. Lee.

The material used for the drops in the following experiments was the highest grade of clock-oil, the density of which, at 23° C., the temperature

---

[1] The pressure p_2 within an oil drop is given by

$$p_2 = k + \frac{\alpha}{2R}$$

where k is LaPlace's constant of internal pressure, α the constant of surface tension and R the radius. The difference $(p_2 - p_1)$ between the pressure within the oil drop and within the oil in bulk is then $\alpha/2R$. But the coefficient of compressibility of a liquid is defined by

$$\beta = \frac{v_2 - v_1}{v_1(p_2 - p_1)}.$$

Now β for oil of this sort never exceeds 70×10^{-6} megadynes per sq. cm. (see Landolt and Bornstein's tables), while α is about 35 dyne cm. R for the smallest drop used (Table XX.) is .00005 cm.; we have then

$$\frac{v_2 - v_1}{v_1} = \beta \frac{\alpha}{2R} = \frac{70 \times 10^{-12} \times 35}{.0001} = .000024.$$

The density of the smallest drop used is then 2 parts in 100,000 greater than that of the oil in bulk. The small drops could then only be appreciably denser than the larger ones if the oil were inhomogeneous and if the atomizing process selected the heavier constituents for the small drops. Such an assumption is negatived by the experimental results given in § 9.

122

ROBERT ANDREWS MILLIKAN

at which the experiments were carried out, was found in two determinations made four months apart, to be .9199 with an error of not more than one part in 10,000.

The electric fields were produced by a 5,300-volt storage battery, the P.D. of which dropped on an average 5 or 10 volts during an observation of an hour's duration. The potential readings were taken, just before and just after a set of observations on a given drop, by dividing the bank into 6 parts and reading the P.D. of each part with a 900-volt Kelvin and White electrostatic voltmeter which showed remarkable constancy and could be read easily, in this part of the scale, with an accuracy of about 1 part in 2,000. This instrument was calibrated by comparison with a 750-volt Weston Laboratory Standard Voltmeter certified correct to 1/10 per cent. and actually found to have this accuracy by comparison with an instrument standardized at the Bureau of Standards in Washington. The readings of P.D. should therefore in no case contain an error of more than 1 part in 1,000. As a matter of fact 5,000 volt readings made with the aid of two different calibration curves of the K. & W. instrument made two years apart never differed by more than 1 or 2 parts in 5,000.

The value of F involves in addition to P.D. the distance between the plates, which was as before 16 mm. and correct to about .01 mm. (l. c., p. 351). Nothing more need be said concerning the first two of the above-mentioned factors. The last four however need especial consideration.

2. THE COEFFICIENT OF VISCOSITY OF AIR.

This factor certainly introduces as large an element of uncertainty as inheres anywhere in the oil-drop method. Since it appears in equation (1) in the 3/2 power an uncertainty of 0.5 per cent. in η means an uncertainty of 0.75 per cent. in e. It was therefore of the utmost importance that η be determined with all possible accuracy. Accordingly two new determinations were begun three years ago in the Ryerson Laboratory, one by Mr. Lachlan Gilchrist and one by Mr. I. M. Rapp. Mr. Gilchrist, whose work has already been published,[1] used a constant deflection method (with concentric cylinders), which it was estimated (l. c., p. 386) ought to reduce the uncertainty in η to 1 or 2 tenths of a per cent. The results have justified this estimate. Mr. Rapp used a form of the capillary tube method which it was thought was better adapted to an *absolute evaluation of* η than have been the capillary tube arrangements which have been commonly used heretofore.[2] Since Mr.

[1] Lachlan Gilchrist, PHYS. REV., 2d Ser., Vol. 1, p. 124.

[2] This investigation will shortly be published in full (PHYS. REV., 1913), hence only a bare statement will here be made of the results which are needed for the problem in hand.

Gilchrist completed his work at the University of Toronto, Canada, and Mr. Rapp made his computations and final reductions at Ursinus College, Pa., neither observer had any knowledge of the results obtained by the other.   The two results agree within 1 part in 600.   Mr. Rapp estimates his maximum uncertainty at 0.1 per cent., Mr. Gilchrist at 0.2 per cent. Mr. Rapp's work was done at 26° C. and gave η_{26} = .00018375.   When this is reduced to 23° C., the temperature used in the following work, by means of formula (5)—a formula[1] which certainly can introduce no appreciable error for the range of temperature here used,—viz.,

$$\eta_t = 0.00018240 - 0.000000493(23 - t); \qquad (5)$$

there results

$$\eta_{23} = .00018227.$$

Mr. Gilchrist's work was done at 20.2° C. and gave $\eta_{20.2}$ = .0001812. When this is reduced to 23° C. it yields

$$\eta_{23} = .00018257.$$

When this new work, by totally dissimilar methods, is compared with the best existing determinations by still other methods the agreement is exceedingly striking.   Thus in 1905, Hogg[2] made at Harvard very careful observations on the damping of oscillating cylinders and obtained in three experiments at atmospheric pressure η_{23} = 0.0001825, $\eta_{15.6}$ = 0.0001790 and $\eta_{18.6}$ = 0.0001795.   These last two reduced to 23° C., as above, are 0.0001826 and 0.0001817 respectively and the mean value of the three determinations is

$$\eta_{23} = 0.00018227.$$

Tomlinson's classical determination,[3] by far the most reliable of the nineteenth century, yielded when the damping was due primarily to "push" $\eta_{12.65° \text{ C.}}$ = 0.00017746; when it was due wholly to "drag" $\eta_{11.79° \text{ C}}$ = 0.00017711.   These values reduced to 15° C., as above, are respectively 0.00017862 and 0.00017867.   Hence we may take Tomlinson's direct determination as η_{15} = 0.00017864.   This reduced to 23° C. by Tomlinson's own temperature formula (Holman's) yields η_{23} = 0.00018242.   By the above formula it yields η_{23} = 0.00018256.

Grindley and Gibson using the tube method on so large a scale[4] (tube 1/8 inch in diameter and 108 feet long) as to largely eliminate the most

---

[1] See R. A. Millikan, Annalen der Physik, 1913, for a more extended discussion of this and other viscosity formulæ and measurements.

[2] J. L. Hogg, Proc. Amer. Acad., 40, 18, p. 611, 1905.

[3] Tomlinson, Phil. Trans., 177, p. 767, 1886.

[4] Grindley and Gibson, Proc. Roy. Soc., 80, p. 114, 1908.

fruitful sources of error in this method, namely, the smallness and un-uniformity of the bore, obtained at room temperature the following results:[1] $\eta_{25.28° \text{ C.}} = .00018347$, $\eta_{23.55° \text{ C.}} = .00018241$, $\eta_{12.18° \text{ C.}} = .00018257$, and $\eta_{15.4° \text{ C.}} = .0001782$. These numbers, reduced to 23° C. as above, are respectively 18,245, 18,241, 18,201, and 18,195. The mean is 18,220. Grindley and Gibson's own formula, $\eta = .0001702 \{1 + .00329t - .0000070t^2\}$, yields $\eta_{23} = .00018245$. We may take then Grindley and Gibson's direct determination as the mean of these two values, viz.: $\eta_{23} = .00018232$.

Collecting then the five most careful determinations of the viscosity of air which so far as I am able to discover have ever been made we obtain the following table.

TABLE I.

Air $\eta_{23} = .00018227$—Rapp. Capillary tube method. 1913.
Air $\eta_{23} = .00018257$—Gilchrist. Constant deflection method. 1913.
Air $\eta_{23} = .00018227$—Hogg. Damping of oscillating cylinder method. 1905.
Air $\eta_{23} = .00018258$—Tomlinson. Damping of pendular vibrations method. 1886.
Air $\eta_{23} = .00018232$—Grindley and Gibson. Flow through large pipe method. 1908.
Mean = **.00018240**

It will be seen, then, that every one of the five different methods which have been used for the absolute determination of η leads to a value which differs by less than 1 part in 1,000 from the above mean value $\eta_{23} = .00018240$. It is surely legitimate then to conclude that the absolute value of η for air is now known with an uncertainty of somewhat less than 1 part in 1,000.[2]

[1] These numbers represent the reduction to absolute C.G.S. units of all the observations which Grindley and Gibson made between 50° F. and 80° F.

[2] In obtaining the above mean I have chosen what, after careful study, I have considered to be the best determination by each of the five distinct methods. The transpiration method has been much more commonly used than have the others, and in general, the final result is in good agreement with other careful work by this method. Thus Rankine's final value (Proc. Roy. Soc., A, 83, p. 522, 1910) by a new modification of the capillary tube method, while probably not claiming an accuracy of more than .4 per cent., is, at 10.6° C., .0001767, a value which reduces to $\eta_{23} = .0001828$. Again Fisher's final formula (PHYS. REV., 28, p. 104, 1909) gives $\eta_{23} = .00018218$. Also Holman's much used formula (Phil. Mag., 21, p. 199, 1886, and Tomlinson, Phil. Trans., Vol. 177, part 2, p. 767, 1886) yields $\eta_{23} = .00018237$. In fact the only reliable work on η which I am able to find which is out of line with the value $\eta_{23} = .00018240$ is that by Breiterbach at Leipzig (Ann. der Phys., 5, p. 166, 1901) and that by Schultze (Ann. der Phys., 5, p. 157, 1901) and several other observers at the University of Halle who used Schultze's apparatus (Markowski, Ann. der Phys., 14, p. 742, 1904, and Tanzler, Verh. der D. Phys. Ges., 8, p. 222, 1906). None of these observers however were aiming at an absolute determination, but rather at the effects of temperature and the mixing of gases upon viscosity and their capillaries were too small (of the order .007 cm.) to make possible an absolute determination of high accuracy. Their agreement among themselves upon a value which is about 1.3 per cent. too high is partly accounted for by the fact that everal of them used the same tube. None of the m made any effort to eliminate the necessarily large error in the measurement of so small a bore (which appears in the result in the fourth power) by taking the mean of η from a considerable number of tubes.

A second question which might be raised in connection with η is as to whether the medium offers precisely the same resistance to the motion through it of a heavily charged drop as to that of an uncharged drop. This question has been carefully studied and definitely answered in the affirmative by the following work (cf. §§ 6 and 10).

3. THE SPEEDS v_1 AND v_2.

The accuracy previously attained in the measurement of the times of ascent and descent between fixed cross-hairs was altogether satisfactory, but the method which had to be employed for finding the magnifying power of the optical system, *i. e.*, for finding the actual distance of fall of the drop in centimeters, left something to be desired. This optical system was before a short-focus telescope of such depth of focus that it was quite impossible to obtain an accurate measure of the distance between the cross-hairs by simply bringing a standard scale into sharp focus immediately after focusing upon a drop. Accordingly, as stated in the original article, the standard scale was set up at the exact distance from the telescope of the pin-hole through which the drop entered the field. This distance could be measured with great accuracy but *the procedure assumed that the drop remained exactly at this distance throughout the whole of any observation, sometimes of several hours duration.* But if there were the slightest lack of parallelism between gravity and the lines of the electric field the drop would be obliged to drift slowly, and always in the same direction, away from this position, and a drift of 5 mm. was enough to introduce an error of 1 per cent. Such a drift could in no way be noticed by the observer if it took place in the line of sight; for the speeds of the drops were changing *very slowly* anyway because of evaporation, fall in the potential of the battery, etc., and a change in time due to such a drift would be completely masked by other causes of change. This source of uncertainty was well recognized at the time of the earlier observations and steps were taken at the beginning of the present work to eliminate it. It was in fact responsible for an error of nearly two per cent.

A new optical system was built, consisting of an achromatic objective of 28 mm. aperture and 12.5 cm. focal length and an eyepiece of 12 mm. focal length. The whole system was mounted in a support which could be moved bodily back and forth by means of a horizontal screw of ½ mm. pitch. In an observation the objective was 25 cm. distant from the drop, which was kept continually in sharp focus by advancing or withdrawing the whole telescope system. The depth of focus was so small that a motion of ½ mm. blurred badly the image of the drop. The eyepiece

was provided with a scale having 80 horizontal divisions and the distance
between the extreme divisions of this scale (the distance of fall in the
following experiments) could be regularly duplicated with an accuracy of
at least 1 part in 1,000, by bringing a standard scale (Société Genevoise)
into sharp focus. (The optical path when the scale was viewed was
made exactly the same as when the drop was viewed.) The distance of
fall, then, one of the most uncertain factors of the preceding determination, was now known with at least this degree of precision.

The accuracy of the *time* determinations can be judged from the data in
Tables IV.–XIX. On account of the great convenience of a direct-reading
instrument these time measurements were all made, not with a chronograph, as heretofore, but with a Hipp chronoscope which read to 0.002
second. This instrument was calibrated by comparison with the standard
Ryerson Laboratory clock under precisely the same conditions as those
under which it was used in the observations themselves and found to have
an error between 0 and 0.2 per cent. depending upon the time interval
measured. For the sake of enabling others to check all the computations herein contained if desired, as well as for the sake of showing what
sort of consistency was attained in the measurement of time intervals
there are given in Table II. the calibration readings for the 30 sec. interval
and in Table III. the results of similar readings for all the intervals used.

TABLE II.   TABLE III.

Chronoscope Readings for 30 Sec. Interval.		Clock Interval, Sec.	Chronoscope Interval.	Corr'n Applied, Per Cent.
29.962	29.990	6	6.0146	−0.26
29.988	29.958	10	10.0018	0.00
29.986	29.920	16	16.0080	0.00
29.930	29.972	20	19.9835	+0.07
29.964	29.976	30	29.9695	+0.10
30.002	30.006	40	39.9436	+0.14
29.940	29.979	60	59.9072	+0.16
29.998	30.018	114	113.795	+0.20
29.930	29.926	120	119.782	+0.20
29.967	29.972			
Corr'n = +.1 per cent.				

The change in the per cent. correction with the time interval employed
is due to the difference in the reaction times of the magnet and spring
contact at make (beginning) and at break (end). All errors of this sort
are obviously completely eliminated by making the calibration observations under precisely the same conditions as the observations on the drop.
In Tables IV. to XIX. the recorded times are the uncorrected chronograph

127

ROBERT ANDREWS MILLIKAN

readings. The corrections are obtained by interpolation in the last column of Table III.

Under the head of possible uncertainties in the velocity determinations are to be mentioned also the effects of a distortion of the drop by the electric field. Such a distortion would increase the surface of the drop, and hence the speed imparted to it per dyne of *electric* force would not be the same as the speed imparted per dyne of gravitational force when the field was off and the drop had the spherical form. The following observations were made in such a way as to bring to light such an effect if it were of sufficient magnitude to exert any influence whatever upon the accuracy of the determination of *e* by this method (cf. §§ 6 and 10).

Similarly objection has been made to the oil-drop method on the ground that, on account of internal convection, fluid drops would not move through air with the same speed as solid drops of like diameter and mass. Such objection is theoretically unjustifiable in the case of oil drops of the sizes here considered.[1] Nevertheless the experimental demonstration of its invalidity is perhaps worth while and is therefore furnished below.

4. THE RADIUS "*a*."

The radius of the drop enters only into the correction term (see equation 4) and so long as this is small need not be determined with a high degree of precision. It is most easily obtained by the following procedure which differs slightly from that originally employed (l. c., p. 379).

It will be seen that the equation (l. c., p. 353)

$$\frac{v_1}{v_2} = \frac{mg}{Fe - mg} \tag{6}$$

contains no assumption whatever save that a given body moves through a given medium with a speed which is proportional to the force acting upon it. Substitution in this equation of $m = \frac{4}{3}\pi a^3(\sigma - \rho)$ and the solution of the resulting equation for *a* gives

$$a = \sqrt[3]{\frac{3Fe}{4\pi g(\sigma - \rho)}\frac{v_1}{(v_1 + v_2)}}. \tag{7}$$

The substitution in this equation of an approximately correct value of *e* yields *a* with an error but one third as great as that contained in the assumed value of *e*. The radius of the drop can then be determined from (7) with a very high degree of precision as *e* becomes more and more accurately known. In the following work the value of *e* substituted in (7) to obtain *a* was 4.78 × 10⁻¹⁰ but the final value of *e* obtained would

[1] Hadamard, Compt. Rendus, 1911.

not have been appreciably different if the value substituted in (7) to obtain *a* had been 5 per cent. or 6 per cent. in error. The determination of *a* therefore introduces no perceptible error into the evaluation of *e*.

5. The Correction-Term Constant A.

This constant was before graphically determined (l. c., p. 379) by plotting the values of $e_1^{\frac{2}{3}}$ as ordinates and those of l/a as abscissæ and observing that if we let $x = l/a$, $y = e_1^{\frac{2}{3}}$ and $y_0 = e^{\frac{2}{3}}$ equation (3) may be written in the form

$$y_0(1 + Ax) = y \qquad (8)$$

or

$$A = \frac{\dfrac{dy}{dx}}{y_0} = \frac{\text{slope}}{y \text{ intercept}}. \qquad (9)$$

Now even if the slope were correctly determined by the former observations all of the above-mentioned sources of error would enter into the value of the intercept and hence would modify the value of A.

As a matter of fact however the accuracy with which the slope itself was determined could be much improved, for with the preceding arrangement it was necessary to make all the observations at atmospheric pressure and the only way of varying l/a was by varying a, *i. e.*, by using drops of different radii. But when a was very small the drops moved exceedingly slowly under gravity and the minutest of residual convection currents produced relatively large errors in the observed speeds, *i. e.*, in e_1. If for example the time of fall over a distance of 2 mm. is 20 minutes it obviously requires an extraordinary degree of stagnancy to prevent a drift in that time of say .2 mm. due to convection. But this would introduce an error of 10 per cent. into e_1. Furthermore with these slow drops Brownian movements introduce errors which can only be eliminated by taking a very large number of readings[1] and this is not in general feasible with such drops. It is quite impossible then by working at a single pressure to obtain from the graph mentioned above a line long enough (l. c., p. 379) to make the determination of its slope a matter of great precision. Accordingly in the new observations the variation of l/a was effected chiefly through the variation of l, *i. e.*, of the pressure p, rather than of a. This made possible not only the accurate evaluation of e, but also the solution of the interesting question as to the law of fall of a given drop through air at reduced pressures.

[1] Fletcher, Phys. Rev., 33, p. 92, 1911.

6. METHOD OF TESTING THE ASSUMPTIONS INVOLVED IN THE OIL-DROP METHOD.

In order to make clear the method of treatment of the following observations a brief consideration of the assumptions underlying the oil-drop method must here be made. These assumptions may be stated thus:

1. The drag which the medium exerts upon a given drop is unaffected by its charge.

2. Under the conditions of observation the oil drops move through the medium essentially as would solid spheres. This assumption may be split into two parts and stated thus: Neither (2a) distortions due to the electric field nor (2b) internal convection within the drop modify appreciably the law of motion of an oil drop.[1]

3. The density of oil droplets is independent of their radius down to $a = .00005$ cm.

Of these assumptions (2a) is the one which needs the most careful experimental test.[2] It will be seen that it is contained in the fundamental equation of the method (see (7)) which may be written in the form

$$e_n = \frac{mg}{Fv_1} (v_1 + v_2). \tag{10}$$

Or still more conveniently in the form

$$e_n = \frac{mgt_g}{F} \left(\frac{1}{t_g} + \frac{1}{t_F} \right), \tag{11}$$

in which t_g and t_F are the respective time intervals required by the drop to fall under gravity and to rise under the field F the distance between the cross-hairs.

In order to see how the assumption under consideration can be tested let us write the corresponding equation after the same drop has caught n' additional units, namely,

$$e_{n+n'} = \frac{mgt_g}{F} \left(\frac{1}{t_g} + \frac{1}{t_F'} \right). \tag{12}$$

The subtraction of (11) from (12) gives

$$e_{n'} = \frac{mgt_g}{F} \left(\frac{1}{t_F'} - \frac{1}{t_F} \right). \tag{13}$$

[1] M. Brillouin has in addition suggested (see p. 149, La Théorie du Rayonnement et les Quanta) that the drops may be distorted by the molecular bombardment, but Einstein's reply (l. c., p. 150) to this suggestion is altogether unanswerable, and, in addition, such a distortion, if it existed, would make the value of e given by the oil-drop method *too small* instead of too large.

[2] Professor Lunn has however subjected it to a theoretical study and has in this way demonstrated its validity (PHYS. REV., XXXV., p. 227, 1912).

Now equations (11) and (12) show, since mgt_0/F remains constant, that as the drop changes charge the successive values of its charge are proportional to the successive values assumed by the quantity $(1/t_g + 1/t_F)$ and the elementary charge itself is obviously this same constant factor mgt_0/F multiplied by *the greatest common divisor* of all these successive values. It is to be observed too that since $1/t_g$ is in these experiments generally large compared to $1/t_F$ the value of this greatest common divisor, which will be denoted by $(1/t_g + 1/t_F)_0$, is determined primarily by the time of fall *under gravity*, and is but little affected by the time in the field. On the other hand equation (13) shows that the greatest common divisor of the various values of $(1/t_F' - 1/t_F)$, which will be designated by $(1/t_F' - 1/t_F)_0$, when multiplied by the same constant factor mgt_0/F, is also the elementary electrical charge. In other words $(1/t_g+1/t_F)_0$ and $(1/t_F' - 1/t_F)_0$ are one and the same quantity, but while the first represents essentially a speed measurement when the field is off, the second represents a speed measurement in a powerful electric field. If then the assumption under consideration is correct we have two independent ways of obtaining the quantity which when multiplied by the constant factor mgt_0/F is the elementary electrical charge, but if on the other hand the distortion of the drop by the field modifies the law of motion of the oil drop through the medium then $(1/t_g + 1/t_F)_0$ and $(1/t_F' - 1/t_F)_0$ will not be the same. Now *a very careful experimental study of the relations of* $(1/t_g + 1/t_F)_0$ *and* $(1/t_F' - 1/t_F)_0$ *shows so perfect agreement that no effect of distortion in changing measurably the value of e can be admitted.*[1] (See Tables IV. to XIX.)

Turning next to assumption (1), this can be tested in three ways, all of which have been tried with negative results. First a drop containing from one up to six or seven elementary charges can be completely discharged and its time of fall under gravity when uncharged compared with its time when charged. Second, the multiple relationships shown in the successive charges carried by a given drop may be very carefully examined. They cannot hold exactly if when the drop is heavily charged it suffers a larger drag from the medium than when it is lightly charged. Third, when drops having widely different charges and different masses are

---

[1] It may be pointed out in passing that the above discussion brings to light a method of obtaining e which is independent of a viscosity measurement; for $(1/t_F' - 1/t_F)_0$ can be obtained for a body which is heavy enough to be weighed upon a micro-balance. Such a body would fall so rapidly that $1/t_g$ could not be measured, but it could be computed from the measurement of $1/t_F'$ and $1/t_F$ and the equation $(1/t_g + 1/t_F')_0 = (1/t_F' - 1/t_F)_0$. Either (12) or (13) could then be solved for e after m had been determined by direct weighing. A consideration of the sources of error in this method shows however that it cannot be made as accurate as the present method which involves the coefficient of viscosity of air.

brought to the same value of l/a by varying the pressure, the value of e_1 (which is proportional to $(v_1 + v_2)_0$), should come out smaller·for the heavily than for the lightly charged drops. The following observations show that this is not the case.

The last criterion is also a test for $(2b)$ for if internal convection modifies the speed of fall of a drop as Perrin wishes to assume that it may,[1] it must play a smaller and smaller rôle as the drop diminishes in size, hence varying l/a by diminishing a cannot be equivalent to varying l/a by increasing l. In other words the value of e_1 obtained from work on a large drop at a low pressure should be different from that obtained from work on a small drop at so high a pressure that l/a has the same value as for the large drop.

Finally if the density of a small drop is greater than that of a large one (see assumption 3) then, for a given value of l/a, the small drop will show a larger value of e_1 than the large one inasmuch as the computation of e_1 is based on a constant value of σ. *The fact, then, that for a given value of l/a the value of e_1 actually comes out independent of the radius or charge of the drops shows conclusively either that no one of these possible sources of error exists, or else that they neutralize one another so that for the purposes of this experiment they do not exist.* That they do not exist at all is shown by the independent theoretical and experimental tests mentioned above. This removes I think every criticism which has been suggested of the oil-drop method of determining e and N.

7. Summary of Improvements in Method.

In order to obtain the consistency shown in the following observations it was found necessary to take much more elaborate precautions to suppress convection currents in the air of the observing chamber than had at first been thought needful.

To recapitulate, then, the improvements which have been introduced into the oil-drop method, consist in (1) a redetermination of η; (2) an improved optical system; (3) an arrangement for observing speeds at all pressures; (4) the more perfect elimination of convection; (5) the experimental proof of the correctness of all the assumptions underlying the method, viz., (a) that a charge does not alter the drag of the medium on the charged body; (b) that the oil drops act essentially like solid spheres; (c) that the density of the oil drops is the same as the density of the oil in bulk.

---

[1] La Théorie du Rayonnement et les Quanta, p. 239—Rapports et Discussions de la Réunion tenue à Bruxelles, Novembre, 1911. Edited by Langevin and de Broglie. Gauthier-Villars.

132

8. The Experimental Arrangements.

The experimental arrangements are shown in Fig. 1. The brass vessel *D* was built for work at all pressures up to 15 atmospheres but since the present observations have to do only with pressures from 76 cm. down these were measured with a very carefully made mercury manometer *m* which at atmospheric pressure gave precisely the same reading as a

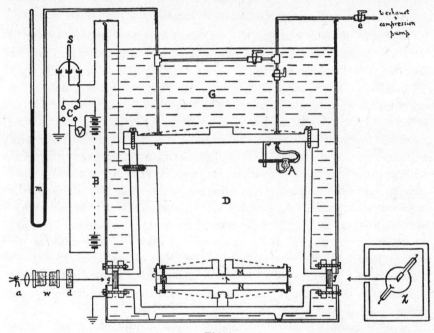

Fig. 1.

standard barometer. Complete stagnancy of the air between the condenser plates *M* and *N* was attained first by absorbing all of the heat rays from the arc *A* by means of a water cell *w*, 80 cm. long, and a cupric chloride cell[1] *d*, and second by immersing the whole vessel *D* in a constant temperature bath *G* of gas-engine oil (40 liters) which permitted, in general, fluctuations of not more than .02° C. during an observation. This constant temperature bath was found essential if such consistency of measurement as is shown below was to be obtained. A long search for causes of slight irregularity revealed nothing so important as this and after the bath was installed all of the irregularities vanished. The atomizer *A* was blown by means of a puff of carefully dried and dust-free air introduced through the cock *e*. The air about the drop *p* was ionized

[1] See Coblentz, Bulletin of the Bureau of Standards, Washington, D. C., Vol. 7, p. 660, 1911.

when desired by means of Röntgen rays from X which readily passed through the glass window g. To the three windows g (two only are shown) in the brass vessel D correspond, of course, three windows in the ebonite strip c which encircles the condenser plates M and N. Through the third of these windows, set at an angle of about 18° from the line Xpa and in the same horizontal plane, the oil drop is observed.

9. The Observations.

The record of a typical set of readings on a given drop is shown in Table IV. The first column, headed t_g, gives the successive readings on the time of descent under gravity. The fourth column, headed t_{F_e} gives the successive times of ascent under the influence of the field F as measured on the Hipp chronoscope. These two columns contain all the data which is used in the computations. But in order to have a test of the stagnancy of the air a number of readings were also made with a stop-watch on the times of ascent through the first half and through the whole distance of ascent. These readings are found in the second and third columns, the times for the first half under the head $\frac{1}{2}t_{F_s}$, the times for the whole distance under the head t_{F_s}. It will be seen from these readings that there is no indication whatever of convection, since the readings for the one half distance have uniformly one half of the value of the readings for the whole distance, within the limits of error of a stop-watch measurement. This sort of a test was made on the majority of the drops, but since no further use is made of these stop-watch readings they will not be given in succeeding tables.

The fifth column, headed $1/t_F$, contains the reciprocals of the values in the fourth column after the correction found from Tables II. and III. has been applied. The sixth column contains the successive differences in the values of $1/t_F$ resulting from the capture of ions. The seventh column, headed n', contains the number of elementary units caught at each change, a number determined simply by observing by what number the quantity just before it in column 6 must be divided to obtain the constancy shown in the eighth column, which contains the successive determinations of $(1/t_F' - 1/t_F)_0$ (see § 6). Similarly the ninth column, headed n, gives the total number of units of charge on the drop, a number determined precisely as in the case of the numbers in the seventh column by observing by what numbers the successive values of $(1/t_g + 1/t_F)$ must be divided to obtain the constancy shown in the tenth column, which contains the successive values of $(1/t_g + 1/t_F)_0$. Since n' is always a small number and in some of the changes almost always has the value 1 or 2 its determination for any change is obviously never a matter of the slightest uncertainty. On the other hand, n is often a large number, but with the aid of the known values of n' it can always be found with absolute certainty so long as it does not exceed say 100 or 150. It will be seen from the means at the bottom of the eighth and the tenth columns that in the case of this drop the two ways discussed in § 6 of obtaining the number which when multiplied by mgt_g/F is the elementary electrical charge yield absolutely identical results.

TABLE IV.

Drop No. 6.

t_g Sec.	$\frac{1}{2}t_{F_e}$ Sec.	t_{F_e} Sec.	t_{F_c} Sec.	$\frac{1}{t_F}$	$\left(\frac{1}{t_{F'}}-\frac{1}{t_F}\right)$	n'	$\frac{1}{n'}\left(\frac{1}{t_{F'}}-\frac{1}{t_F}\right)$	n	$\frac{1}{n}\left(\frac{1}{t_g}+\frac{1}{t_F}\right)$
11.848	39.9	80.2	80.708	.01236				18	.005366
11.890	11.2	22.4	22.366		.03234	6	.005390		
11.908			22.390	.04470				24	.005371
11.904	11.2	22.4	22.368		.03751	7	.005358		
11.882	70.6	140.4	140.565	.007192	.005348	1	.005348	17	.005375
11.906	39.9	79.6	79.600	.01254				18	.005374
11.838			34.748		.01616	3	.005387		
11.816			34.762	.02870				21	.005376
11.776			34.846						
11.840			29.286						.005379
11.904	14.6	29.3	29.236	.03414	.026872	5	.005375	22	
11.870	69.3	137.4	137.308	.007268	.021572	4	.005393	17	.005380
11.952	17.6	34.9	34.638	.02884				21	.005382
11.860					.01623	3	.005410		
11.846			22.104	.04507				24	.005386
11.912			22.268		.04307	8	.005384		
11.910			500.1	.002000				16	.005387
11.918			19.704	.05079	.04879	9	.005421	25	.005399
11.870			19.668		.03874	7	.005401		
11.888			77.630	.01285				18	.005390
11.894	38.9	77.6	77.806		.01079	2	.005395	20	.005392
11.878	21.0	42.6	42.302	.02364					
11.880					Means		**.005386**		**.005384**

Duration of exp. = 45 min.,
Plate distance = 16 mm.,
Fall distance = 10.21 mm.,
Initial volts = 5,088.8.
Final volts = 5,081.2.
Temperature = 22.82° C.,
Pressure = 75.62 cm.,
Oil density = .9199,
Air viscosity[1] = 1,824 × 10⁻⁷,
Radius (a) = .000276 cm.,
l/a = .034,
Speed of fall = .08584 cm./sec.,
$e_1 = 4.991 \times 10^{-10}$.

[1] In the above and in all the following tables the computations were made on the basis of the assumption $\eta_{23} = 1,825 \times 10^{-7}$ instead of $\eta_{23} = 1,824 \times 10^{-7}$ (see § 2). The reduction to the latter value has been made only in the final value of e (see § 10).

TABLE V.
Drop No. 16.

t_g	t_F	$\dfrac{1}{t_F}$	n'	$\dfrac{1}{n'}\left(\dfrac{1}{t'_F}-\dfrac{1}{t_F}\right)$	n	$\dfrac{1}{n}\left(\dfrac{1}{t_g}+\dfrac{1}{t_F}\right)$	
18.638							
18.686							
18.689	17.756 ⎤	.05628 ⎫			16	.006853	
18.730	17.778 ⎦		5	.006908			$V_i = 5106$
18.686	45.978 ⎤	.02174 ⎭			11	.006832	$V_f = 5100$
18.726	45.870 ⎦						$t = 23.7°$ C.
18.772	45.716 ⎤	.021826 ⎫	3	.006795	8	.006851	$p = 74.68$
18.740	45.758 ⎦						$v_1 = .05449$
18.724	694.0	.001441	5	.006860	13	.006855	$a = .0002188$
18.720	27.95	.03574	4	.006825	9	.006868	$l/a = .04390$
18.816	118.388	.008439	2	.006866	11	.006867	$e_1 = 5.065$
18.816	45.030	.02217					
18.716	34.564	.02890			12	.006856	
18.804	44.826	.02227			11	.006876	
18.746	117.198	.008518	2	.006876	9	.006876	
18.746	44.784	.022295	2	.006889	11	.006879	
18.790							
18.738				**.006860**		**.006861**	

TABLE VI.
Drop No. 14.

t_g	t_F	$\dfrac{1}{t_F}$	n'	$\dfrac{1}{n'}\left(\dfrac{1}{t'_F}-\dfrac{1}{t_F}\right)$	n	$\dfrac{1}{n}\left(\dfrac{1}{t_g}+\dfrac{1}{t_F}\right)$	
18.606							
18.732							
18.784							
18.700	46.172	.02163 ⎫			11	.006820	
18.730	17.896 ⎤	.05600	5	.006874			$V_i = 5077$
18.652	17.818 ⎦				16	.006833	$V_f = 5073$
18.656	46.328 ⎤		5	.006886			$t = 23.09°$ C.
18.730	46.258	.02157			11	.006815	$p = 75.28$
18.760	46.266 ⎦		1	.006803			$v_1 = .05451$
18.708	67.473 ⎤						$a = .0002185$
18.658	67.148	.01484			10	.006823	$l/a = .04348$
18.668	67.148 ⎦		6	.006840			$e_1 = 5.064$
18.826	17.896	.05588			16	.006831	
18.710	15.868 ⎤	.06305			17	.006850	
18.802	15.854 ⎦		9	.006853			
18.778	730.0	.001370	6	.006882	8	.006845	
18.790	23.376 ⎤	.04266			14	.006861	
18.846	23.504 ⎦		4	.006850			
18.804	65.416	.01526			10	.006865	
18.662	118.970	.008389	1	.006871	9	.006864	
18.704	622.8	.001605	1	.006784	8	.006874	
18.730				**.006850**		**.006844**	

136

ROBERT ANDREWS MILLIKAN

We omit pp. 126-132, in which Millikan presents figures for twelve other drops and shows the striking consistency of the results obtained from different drops.

Table XX. contains a complete summary of the results obtained on all of the 58 different drops upon which complete series of observations like the above were made during a period of 60 consecutive days. It will be seen from this table that these observations represent a 30-fold variation in l/a (from .016, drop No. 1, to .444, drop No. 58), a 17-fold variation in p (from 4.46 cm., drop No. 56, to 76.27 cm., drop No. 10), a 12-fold variation in a (from 4.69 × 10⁻⁵ cm., drop No. 28, to 58.56 × 10⁻⁵ cm., drop No. 1) and a variation in the number of free electrons carried by the drop from 1 on drop No. 28 to 136 on drop No. 56. The time of fall of drop No. 28 was also tested when it was completely discharged, as have been the times of many other drops which carried most of the time but one electron.

Much larger variations both in a and p, and therefore in l/a, might have been used, and have in fact been used, for finding the law of fall of a drop through rarefied air, but for the end here sought, namely, the most accurate possible determination of e, it was found desirable to keep the t_g interval for the most part between the limits 10 sec. and 40 sec., in order to avoid chronograph errors on the one hand and Brownian movement irregularities on the other. That neither of these sources of error is appreciable in these observations may be seen from a study of Tables IV.–XIX., which are thoroughly representative of the work on all the drops.

10. Results and Discussion.

It will be seen at once from equation (4) that the value of e is simply the value of e_1 for which $l/a = 0$, so that if successive values of $e_1^{\frac{2}{3}}$ are plotted as abscissæ and of l/a as ordinates the intercept of the resulting curve on the $e_1^{\frac{2}{3}}$ axis is $e^{\frac{2}{3}}$. Furthermore if A is a constant then the curve in question is a straight line and A is the slope of this line divided by the

TABLE XX.

No.	Tem. °C.	P.D. (Volts).	t_g (Sec.).	l_i cm./sec.	$(V_1+V_2)_0$	n	$a\times10^5$ cm.	p (cm. Hg.).	$1/pn$	l/a	$r_1\times10^{10}$	$r_1^{\frac{3}{2}}\times10^8$	$e_i^{\frac{2}{3}}\times10^8$
1	23.00	5,168	4.363	.2357	.003293	77–102	58.56	75.80	22.52	.01615	4.877	61.90	61.14
2	22.80	5,120	8.492	.1202	.004670	27–36	32.64	75.00	40.85	.02933	4.981	62.82	61.26
3	23.46	5,100	9.905	.1032	.004996	22–27	30.29	73.71	44.88	.03212	4.971	62.75	61.04
4	22.85	5,163	10.758	.09489	.005211	18–36	28.94	75.20	45.92	.03288	5.001	63.00	61.24
5	23.08	5,072	10.663	.09575	.005176	20–30	29.14	73.25	46.85	.03353	4.982	62.82	61.13
6	22.82	5,085	11.880	.08584	.005497	17–24	27.54	75.62	48.11	.03437	4.991	62.93	61.09
7	23.79	5,090	11.950	.08368	.005480	19–22	27.57	75.10	48.44	.03466	4.981	62.82	61.07
8	23.50	5,158	12.540	.08141	.005623	16–19	26.90	75.30	49.52	.03544	5.016	63.12	61.23
9	22.87	5,139	13.562	.07375	.005962	19–23	25.71	75.00	51.73	.03702	5.016	63.13	61.15
10	23.25	5,015	15.380	.06641	.006174	13–22	24.31	76.27	54.09	.03871	5.010	63.08	61.02
11	23.01	5,066	15.193	.06720	.006087	11–14	24.36	73.90	55.52	.03973	5.015	63.12	61.00
12	23.00	5,080	15.985	.06375	.006416	12–16	23.70	75.14	56.15	.04018	5.028	63.24	61.10
13	23.00	5,024	15.695	.05463	.006873	9–15	21.91	76.06	59.94	.04290	5.043	63.35	61.06
14	23.09	5,077	18.730	.05451	.006988	8–16	21.85	75.28	60.78	.04348	5.064	63.53	61.21
15	23.85	5,078	18.959	.05274	.006966	8–18	21.78	75.24	61.03	.04368	5.040	63.33	61.07
16	23.70	5,103	18.738	.05449	.007005	9–16	21.87	74.68	61.33	.04390	5.065	63.54	61.21
17	23.06	5,060	18.415	.05545	.006890	9–18	22.06	73.47	61.69	.04411	5.054	63.43	61.00
18	22.83	5,093	26.130	.03907	.008339	5–13	18.45	75.54	71.74	.05134	5.098	63.82	61.08
19	22.95	5,033	28.568	.03570	.008651	5–9	17.63	75.87	74.77	.05350	5.120	64.00	61.12
20	23.00	5,094	9.480	.10772	.005058	23–32	30.54	41.77	78.40	.05612	5.145	64.22	61.23
21	23.08	5,018	35.253	.02893	.009660	4–11	15.80	74.32	85.08	.06089	5.166	64.36	61.11
22	23.22	5,005	40.542	.02515	.010332	3–9	14.75	76.42	88.70	.06350	5.168	64.40	61.01
23	22.76	5,098	39.900	.02554	.010510	3–6	14.85	75.40	89.35	.06395	5.190	64.59	61.18
24	23.16	5,050	12.466	.08189	.005896	15–28	26.44	37.19	101.8	.07283	5.269	65.24	61.35
25	22.98	5,066	15.157	.06737	.006399	12–17	24.01	38.95	107.2	.07660	5.278	65.28	61.20
26	23.20	4,572	7.875	.12980	.004324	33–40	33.07	24.33	124.4	.08892	5.379	66.06	61.31
27	23.18	4,570	9.408	.1085	.004730	23–29	30.23	25.37	130.4	.09330	5.381	66.16	61.18
28	23.00	5,145	84.270	.1211	.01595	1–4	4.69	75.83	130.3	.09322	5.379	66.14	61.16
29	22.99	5,073	23.223	.04393	.008488	6–12	19.06	33.47	156.8	.1117	5.529	67.36	61.37

Mean = 61.120

Mean = 61.138

No.	Tem. °C.	P.D. (Volts).	t_g (Sec.).	V_1 cm./sec.	$(V_1+V_2)_0$	n	$a \times 10^5$ cm.	l (cm. Hg).	$1/p_a$	l/a	$e_1 \times 10^{10}$	$e_1^{2/3} \times 10^8$	$e^{2/3} \times 10^8$
30	23.19	5,090	26.830	.03801	.009111	5–10	17.77	35.18	160.2	.1147	5.507	67.18	61.06
31	22.89	5,098	38.479	.02649	.011180	3–5	14.71	36.51	176.5	.1263	5.621	68.12	61.38
32	23.06	5,070	14.060	.07246	.006762	12–17	24.29	21.12	195.0	.1394	5.692	68.67	61.22
33	23.07	4,582	18.229	.05601	.006981	10–13	21.33	23.86	196.6	.1405	5.687	68.64	61.13
34	23.06	5,061	38.010	.02682	.011205	3–8	14.72	34.01	199.8	.1429	5.714	68.84	61.20
35	23.00	4,246	9.265	.11032	.004653	27–34	29.84	16.00	209.5	.1499	5.739	69.07	61.07
36	22.91	4,236	9.879	.10340	.004863	24–28	28.74	15.67	222.0	.1589	5.820	69.71	61.23
37	23.06	4,236	12.040	.08496	.005362	18–24	26.27	16.75	227.5	.1625	5.821	69.72	61.03
38	22.94	2,556	10.657	.09581	.003109	32–43	27.49	14.70	247.5	.1771	5.935	70.61	61.16
39	23.00	5,054	19.950	.05115	.008370	8–15	20.12	19.73	251.8	.1802	5.910	70.41	60.79
40	23.09	5,058	21.130	.04830	.008865	7–9	18.38	18.54	278.3	.1993	6.076	71.72	61.09
41	23.05	5,062	24.008	.04254	.009496	6–8	18.16	19.01	289.6	.2073	6.110	72.03	60.97
42	22.94	4,238	18.347	.05564	.007110	9–17	20.60	15.72	308.8	.2210	6.224	73.04	61.24
43	23.18	3,254	13.909	.07340	.004729	16–28	23.70	13.55	311.0	.2227	6.214	72.83	60.95
44	23.04	4,231	29.114	.03503	.009273	5–9	16.16	17.17	360.6	.2579	6.466	74.77	61.00
45	22.97	3,317	29.776	.03425	.007430	5–12	15.90	17.27	364.2	.2606	6.537	75.30	61.39
46	22.81	3,401	25.909	.03937	.007311	6–19	16.90	14.68	403.3	.2886	6.719	76.71	61.30
47	22.83	2,550	12.891	.07921	.003935	18–42	23.80	9.70	432.8	.3097	6.841	77.66	61.13
48	22.80	2,559	32.326	.03150	.006286	7–14	15.01	15.35	433.8	.3104	6.866	77.85	61.28
49	23.02	3,370	14.983	.06815	.011353	8–9	22.00	10.10	448.8	.3221	6.936	78.36	61.22
50	23.45	2,535	11.659	.08757	.003783	25–30	24.88	8.60	466.7	.3340	6.978	78.67	60.85
51	23.48	2,539	10.924	.09346	.003615	27–34	25.69	8.26	470.7	.3368	7.024	79.02	61.04
52	22.98	3,351	50.400	.02021	.010775	2–6	11.83	16.95	498.5	.3568	7.210	80.40	61.36
53	23.16	2,451	33.379	.03055	.006623	5–10	14.39	12.61	551.3	.3945	7.470	82.19	61.13
54	23.46	2,533	19.227	.05347	.005314	11–17	18.87	9.03	587.8	.4112	7.661	83.73	61.18
55	22.90	2,546	24.254	.04206	.006041	9–18	16.72	10.11	591.5	.4233	7.672	83.82	61.22
56	23.21	1,700	5.058	.20256	.001861	117–136	36.53	4.46	614.2	.4396	7.777	84.57	61.11
57	23.12	2,321	15.473	.06599	.004360	18–24	20.85	7.74	619.7	.4435	7.774	84.54	60.87
58	23.03	3,388.5	24.33	.04196	.008183	6–10	16.62	9.070	620.2	.4439	7.810	84.83	61.14

Mean = 61.138

Mean of all numbers in last column = 61.138
Mean of first 23 numbers = 61.120

139

ROBERT ANDREWS MILLIKAN

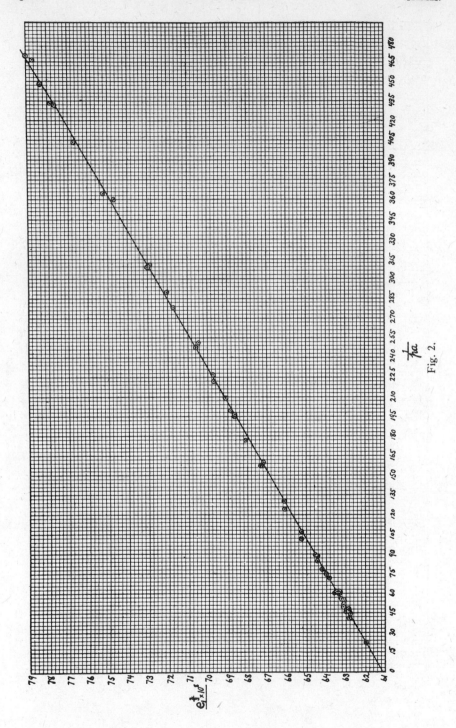

Fig. 2.

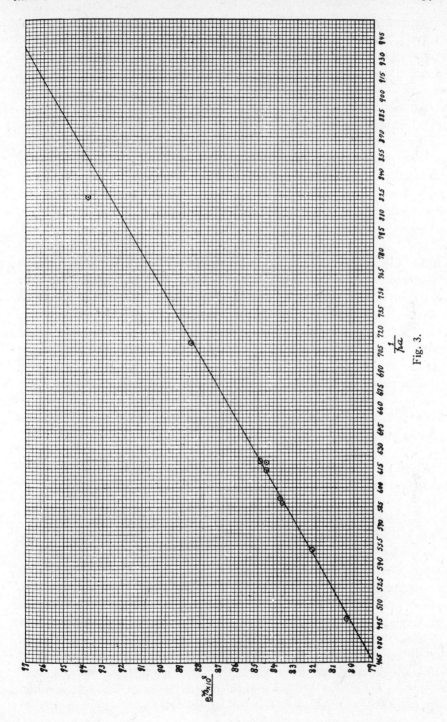

$\dfrac{1}{na}$

Fig. 3.

y intercept (see equation 9). In view of the uncertainty in l due to the fact that k in the equation $\eta = knm\bar{c}l$ has never been exactly evaluated, it was thought preferable to write the correction term to Stokes's law (see (2 and 3) in the form $(1 + b/pa)^{-1}$ instead of in the form $(1 + Al/a)^{-1}$ and then to plot $e_1{}^{\frac{2}{3}}$ against $1/pa$. Nevertheless in view of the greater ease of visualization of l/a all the values of this quantity corresponding to successive values of $1/pa$ are given in Table XX., k being taken, merely for the purposes of this computation, as .3502 (Boltzmann). Fig. 2 shows the graph obtained by plotting the values of $e_1{}^{\frac{2}{3}}$ against $1/pa$ for the first 51 drops of Table XX., and Fig. 3 shows the extension of this graph to twice as large values of $1/pa$ and $e_1{}^{\frac{2}{3}}$. It will be seen that there is not the slightest indication of a departure from a linear relation between $e_1{}^{\frac{2}{3}}$ and $1/pa$ up to the value $1/pa = 620.2$ which corresponds to a value of l/a of .4439 (see drop No. 58, Table XX.). Furthermore the scale used in the plotting is such that a point which is one division above or below the line in Fig. 2 represents in the mean an error of 2 in 700. *It will be seen from Figs. 2 and 3 that there is but one drop in the 58 whose departure from the line amounts to as much as 0.5 per cent. It is to be remarked, too, that this is not a selected group of drops but represents all of the drops experimented upon during 60 consecutive days,* during which time the apparatus was taken down several times and set up anew. It is certain then that an equation of the form (2) holds very accurately up to $l/a = .4$. The last drop in Fig. 3 seems to indicate the beginning of a departure from this linear relationship. Since such departure has no bearing upon the evaluation of e, discussion of it wil be postponed to another paper.

Attention may also be called to the completeness of the answers furnished by Figs. 2 and 3 to the questions raised in § 6. Thus drops No. 27 and 28 have practically identical values of $1/pa$ but while No. 28 carries, during part of the time, but 1 unit of charge (see Table XX.) drop No. 27 carries 29 times as much and it has about 7 times as large a diameter. Now if the small drop were denser than the large one (see assumption 3, § 6) or if the drag of the median upon the heavily charged drop were greater than its drag upon the one lightly charged (see assumtion 1, § 6), then for both these reasons drop 27 would move more slowly relatively to drop 28 then would otherwise be the case and hence $e_1{}^{\frac{2}{3}}$ for 27 would fall below $e_1{}^{\frac{2}{3}}$ for drop 28. Instead of this the two $e_1{}^{\frac{2}{3}}$'s fall so nearly together that it is impossible to represent them on the present scale by two separate dots. Drops 52 and 56 furnish an even more striking confirmation of the same conclusion, for both drops have about the same value for l/a and both are exactly on the line though No. 56

carries at one time 68 times as heavy a charge as No. 52 and has three times as large a radius. In general the fact that Figs. 2 and 3 show no tendency whatever on the part of either the very small or the very large drops to fall above or below the line is experimental proof of the joint correctness of assumptions 1, 3, and 2b of § 6. The correctness of 2a was shown by the agreement throughout Tables IV. to XIX. between $1/n'(1/t_F' - 1/t_F)$ and $1/n(1/t_g + 1/t_F)$.

The values of $e^{\frac{2}{3}}$ and b obtained graphically from the y-intercept and the slope in Fig. 2 are $e^{\frac{2}{3}} = 61.13 \times 10^{-8}$ and $b = .0006254$, p being measured, for the purposes of Fig. 2 and of this computation in mm. of Hg at 23° C. and a being measured in cm. The value of A (equations 2 and 3) corresponding to this value of B is *.874* instead of *.817* as originally found. Cunningham's theory gives, in terms of the constants here used, $A = 788$.[1]

Instead however of taking the result of this graphical evaluation of $e^{\frac{2}{3}}$ it is more accurate to reduce each of the observations on $e_1^{\frac{2}{3}}$ to $e^{\frac{2}{3}}$ by means of the above value of B and the equation

$$e^{\frac{2}{3}}\left(1 + \frac{b}{pa}\right) = e_1^{\frac{2}{3}}. \qquad (14)$$

The results of this reduction are contained in the last column of Table XX. These results illustrate very clearly the sort of consistency obtained in these observations. *The largest departure from the mean value found anywhere in the table amounts to 0.5 per cent., and "the probable error" of the final mean value computed in the usual way is 16 in 61,000.*

Instead however of using this final mean value as the most reliable evaluation of $e^{\frac{2}{3}}$ it was thought preferable to make a considerable number of observations at atmospheric pressure on drops small enough to make t_g determinable with great accuracy and yet large enough so that the whole correction term to Stokes's law amounted to but a few per cent., since in this case, even, though there might be a considerable error in the correction-term constant b, such error would influence the final value of e by an inappreciable amount. The first 23 drops of Table XX. represent such observations. It will be seen that they show slightly greater consistency than do the remaining drops in the table and that the correction-term reductions for these drops all lie between 1.3 per cent. (drop No. 1) and 5.6 per cent. (drop No. 23) so that even though b were in error by as much as 3 per cent. (its error is actually not more than .5 per cent.) $e^{\frac{2}{3}}$ would be influenced by that fact to the extent of but 0.1 per cent. The mean value of $e^{\frac{2}{3}}$ obtained from the first 23 drops is 61.12×10^{-8}, a

[1] PHYS. REV., 32, p. 380; also footnote.

number which differs by 1 part in 3,400 from the mean obtained from all the drops.

When correction is made for the fact that the numbers in Table XX. were obtained on the basis of the assumption $\eta_{23} = 0001825$, instead of $\eta_{23} = .0001824$ (see § 2) the final mean value of $e^{\frac{3}{2}}$ obtained from the first 23 drops is 61.085×10^{-8}. This corresponds to

$$e = 4.774 \times 10^{-10} \text{ electrostatic units.}$$

Since the value of the Faraday constant has now been fixed virtually by international agreement[1] at 9,650 absolute electromagnetic units and since this is the number N of molecules in a gram molecule times the elementary electrical charge, we have

$$N \times 4.774 \times 10^{-10} = 9,650 \times 2.9990 \times 10^{10};$$

$$\therefore \quad N = 6.062 \times 10^{23}.$$

Although the probable error in this number computed by the method of least squares from Table XX. is but one part in 3,000 it would be erroneous to infer that e and N are now known with that degree of precision, for there are four constant factors entering into all of the results in Table XX. and introducing uncertainties as follows. The coefficient of viscosity η which appears in the $3/2$ power introduces into e and N a maximum possible uncertainty of 0.1 per cent. The distance between the condenser plates (16.00 mm.) is correct to .01 mm., and therefore, since it appears in the 1st power in e, introduces a maximum possible error of something less than 0.1 per cent. The voltmeter readings have a maximum possible error of rather less than 0.1 per cent., and carry this in the 1st power into e and N. The cross-hair distance which is uniformly duplicatable to one part in a thousand appears in the $3/2$ power and introduces an uncertainty of no more than 0.1 per cent. The other factors introduce errors which are negligible in comparison. *The uncertainty in e and N is then that due to 4 continuous factors each of which introduces a maximum possible uncertainty of 0.1 per cent.* Following the usual procedure we may estimate the uncertainty in e and N as the square root of the sum of the squares of these four uncertainties, that is, as 2 parts in 1,000. We have then finally:

$$e = 4.774 \pm .009 \times 10^{-10}$$

and

$$N = 6.062 \pm .012 \times 10^{23}.$$

The difference between these numbers and those originally found by the oil-drop method, viz., $e = 4.891$ and $N = 5.992$ is due to the fact

[1] Atomic weight of silver 107.88. Electrochemical equivalent of silver 0.01118.

that this much more elaborate and prolonged study has had the effect of changing every one of the three factors η, A, and d ($=$ cross-hair distance) in such a way as to lower e and to raise N. The chief change however has been due to the elimination of the faults of the original optical system.

11. Comparison with Other Measurements.

So far as I am aware, there is at present no determination of e or N by any other method which does not involve an uncertainty at least 15 times as great as that represented in the above measurements.

Thus the *radioactive method* yields in the hands of Regener[1] a count of the α particles which gives e with an uncertainty which he estimates at 3 per cent. This is as high a precision I think as has yet been claimed for any α particle count,[2] though Geiger and Rutherford's photographic registration[3] method will doubtless be able to improve it.

The *Brownian Movement* method yields results which fluctuate between Perrin's value[4] $e = 4.24 \times 10^{-10}$, and Fletcher's value,[5] 5.01×10^{-10}, with Svedberg's measurements[6] yielding the intermediate number 4.7×10^{-10}.

The *radiation method* of Planck[7] yields N as a product of $(c_2)^3$ and σ. The latest Reichsanstalt value of c_2 is 1.436[8] while Coblentz,[9] as the result of extraordinarily careful and prolonged measurements obtains 1.4456. The difference in these two values of $(c_2)^3$ is 2 per cent. Westphal[10] estimates his error in the measurement of σ at .5 per cent. though reliable observers differ in it by 5 per cent. or 6 per cent. We may take then 3 per cent. as the limit of accuracy thus far attained in measurements of e or N by other methods. *The mean results by each one of the three other methods fall well within this limit of the value found above by the oil-drop method.*

12. Computation of Other Fundamental Constants.

For the sake of comparison and reference, the following fundamental constants are recomputed on the basis of the above measurements:

[1] Regener, Sitz. Ber. d. k. Preuss. Acad., 37, p. 948, 1909.

[2] Rutherford and Geiger, Proc. Roy. Soc., 81, p. 155, 1908.

[3] Gciger and Rutherford, Phil. Mag., 24, p. 618, 1912.

[4] J. Perrin, C. R., 152, p. 1165, 1911.

[5] H. Fletcher, Phys. Rev., 33, p. 107, 1911.

[6] Svedberg, Arkiv f. Kemi, etc., utg. af K. Sv. Vetensk. Akad., 2, 29, 1906. See also Svedberg, "Die Existenz der Mölekule," p. 136. Leipzig, 1912.

[7] Planck, Vorlesungen über die Theorie der Wärmestrahlung, 2d edition, 1913, p. 166.

[8] See Planck, Vorles., p. 163.

[9] Coblentz, Journal of the Washington Academy of Sciences, Vol. 3, p. 178, April, 1913.

[10] Wm. H. Westphal, Verh. d. D. Phys. Ges., 13, p. 987, Dec., 1912.

ROBERT ANDREWS MILLIKAN

1. The number n of molecules in 1 c.c. of an ideal gas at $0°$ 76 is given by

$$n = \frac{N}{V} = \frac{6.062 \times 10^{23}}{22,412} = 2.705 \times 10^{19}.$$

2. The mean kinetic energy of agitation E_0 of a molecule at $0°$ C. is given by

$$pV = \tfrac{1}{3}Nmu^2 = \tfrac{2}{3}NE_0 = RT,$$

$$\therefore E_0 = \frac{3}{2}\frac{p_0V_0}{N} = \frac{3 \times 1,013,700 \times 22,412}{2 \times 6.062 \times 10^{23}} = 5.621 \times 10^{-14} \text{ ergs.}$$

3. The constant ϵ of molecular energy defined by $E_0 = \epsilon T$ is given by

$$\epsilon = \frac{E_0}{T} = \frac{5.621 \times 10^{-14}}{273.11} = 2.058 \times 10^{-16} \frac{\text{ergs}}{\text{degrees}}.$$

4. The Boltzmann entropy constant k defined by $S = k \log W$ is given by[1]

$$k = \frac{R}{N} = \frac{p_0V_0}{TN} = \tfrac{2}{3}\epsilon = 1.372 \times 10^{-16} \frac{\text{ergs}}{\text{degrees}}.$$

All of these constants are known with precisely the accuracy attained in the measurement of e.

5. The Planck "Wirkungsquantum" h can probably be obtained considerably more accurately as follows than in any other way. From equation 292, p. 166, of the "Wärmestrahlung," we obtain[2]

$$h = \frac{k^{\frac{4}{3}}}{c}\left(\frac{48\pi\alpha}{a}\right)^{\frac{1}{3}} = \frac{(1.372 \times 10^{-16})^{\frac{4}{3}}}{2.999 \times 10^{10}} \cdot \left(\frac{48\pi 1.0823}{7.39 \times 10^{-15}}\right)^{\frac{1}{3}} = 6.620 \times 10^{-27}$$

which gives h with the same accuracy attainable in the measurement of $k^{\frac{4}{3}}/a$ in which a is the Stefan-Boltzmann constant. If Westphal's estimate of his error in the measurement of this constant is correct, viz., 0.5 per cent., it would introduce an uncertainty of but 0.2 per cent. into h. This is about that introduced by the above determination of $k^{\frac{4}{3}}$, hence the above value of h should not be in error by more than 0.4 per cent.

6. The constant c_2 of the Wien-Planck radiation law may also be computed with much precision from the above measurements. For also from equation 292 of the "Wärmestrahlung" we obtain

$$c_2 = \left(\frac{48\pi\alpha k}{a}\right)^{\frac{1}{3}} = \left(\frac{48\pi 1.0823 \ 1.372 \times 10^{-16}}{7.39 \times 10^{-15}}\right)^{\frac{1}{3}} = 1.4470 \text{ cm. degrees.}$$

[1] See Planck's Vorles., p. 129.

[2] c = velocity of light, α = a numerical factor, and $a = 4\sigma/c$. Westphal's value of σ is 5.54×10^{-5} which corresponds to $a = 7.39 \times 10^{-15}$.

Since both k and a here appear in the 1/3 power, the error in c should be no more than 0.2 per cent., provided Westphal's error is no more than 0.5 per cent.

The difference between this and Coblentz's mean value, viz., *1.4456* is but 0.1 per cent. The agreement is then entirely satisfactory. A further independent check is found in the fact that Day and Sosman's location of the melting point of platinum at 1755° C.[1] is equivalent to a value of $c_2 = 1.4475$.[2] On the other hand, the last Reichsanstalt value of c_2, viz., 1.437, is too low to fit well with these and Westphal's measurements. It fits perfectly however with a combination of the above value of e and Shakespear's[3] value of σ, viz., $\sigma = 5.67 \times 10^{-5}$.

13. Summary.

The results of this work may be summarized in the following table in which the numbers in the error column represent in the case of the first six numbers estimated limits of uncertainty rather than the so-called "probable errors" which would be much smaller. The last two constants however involve Westphal's measurements and estimates and Planck's equations as well as my own observations.

Table XXI.

Elementary electrical charge..........................	$e = 4.774 \pm .009 \times 10^{-10}$
Number of molecules per gram molecule............	$N = 6.062 \pm .012 \times 10^{23}$
Number of gas molecules per c.c. at 0° 76..........	$n = 2.705 \pm .005 \times 10^{19}$
Kinetic energy of a molecule at 0° C...............	$E_0 = 5.621 \pm .010 \times 10^{-4}$
Constant of molecular energy......................	$\epsilon = 2.058 \pm .004 \times 10^{-16}$
Constant of the entropy equation...................	$k = 1.372 \pm .002 \times 10^{-16}$
Elementary "Wirkungsquantum"....................	$h = 6.620 \pm .025 \times 10^{-27}$
Constant of the Wien displacement law.............	$c_2 = 1.4470 \pm 0030$

I take pleasure in acknowledging the able assistance of Mr. J. Yinbong Lee in making some of the above observations. Mr. Lee has also repeated with my apparatus the observations on oil at atmospheric pressure with results which are nearly as consistent as the above. Using my value of b he obtains, as a mean of measurements on 14 drops, a value of e which differs from the above by less than 1 part in 6,000, although its probable error computed as in the case of Table XX. is 1 part in 2,000.

Ryerson Physical Laboratory,
    University of Chicago,
        June 2, 1913.

[1] Amer. Jour. Sci., 30, p. 3, 1910.
[2] Coblentz, Journal of the Washington Academy of Sciences, Vol. 3, p. 13.
[3] G. A. Shakespear, Proc. Roy. Soc., 86, 180, 1911.

ROBERT ANDREWS MILLIKAN

ARTHUR
HOLLY
COMPTON

1892-1962

When Arthur Compton graduated from college he considered taking up a religious career. But his father advised him that he ought to go into science: "Your work in this field may become a more valuable Christian service than if you were to enter the ministry or become a missionary." Such thoughts helped Compton reconcile the two chief influences of his upbringing, devout religion and intellectual work. His father was Professor of Philosophy and later Dean of the College of Wooster, where Arthur was educated; his older brother and good friend Karl, later a noted physicist and president of the Massachusetts Institute of Technology, communicated his own love of science.

At an early point Karl introduced Arthur to the study of X-rays, which was to be the younger brother's main line of work for many years. In 1913 he followed Karl to Princeton, and for his Ph.D. thesis studied the angular distribution of X-rays reflected from crystals. On graduation in 1916 he married a classmate from Wooster College, Betty McCloskey, who became an intelligent and enthusiastic partner in his later activities. Compton was named instructor in physics at the University of Minnesota, one of a number of state-supported schools that were working hard to teach science and to introduce the spirit of pure research. The experiments begun here eventually led Compton to state that magnetization of a material depends not on the orbits of the electrons in it, but on the electron's own elementary characteristics; he was the first to suggest the existence of quantized electron spin.

Meanwhile he found a job in industry. Engineering had always attracted him, and in 1917 he took a well-paid position as research engineer for Westinghouse. In this work (and in later work helping General Electric develop fluorescent lighting) Compton was starting on a path that many American physicists followed. Industrial laboratories were growing even more rapidly than academic ones; before World

War I industry employed less than 10 percent of the members of The American Physical Society, and not long after, 25 percent.

In 1919 Compton was awarded one of the first National Research Council fellowships. These gave many American physicists of the 1920's and 1930's a chance to study as they chose, and for Compton this meant X-rays. He took his fellowship to the Cavendish Laboratory in England. But the X-ray apparatus there turned out to be inadequate, so he worked on allied problems with gamma rays. He conclusively verified earlier studies by others that showed puzzling variations of wavelength with scattering angle. Back in the United States as head of the physics department in Washington University, St. Louis, Compton pursued this problem, now working again with X-rays. Since his childhood he had possessed great self-confidence, manual skill, ingenuity and patience. All these combined to help him perfect his apparatus and measure the shift of wavelength with scattering angle that is now known as the Compton effect. Studying this result, he carefully considered and eliminated various attempts at classical explanation. In late 1922 he hit upon the stunningly simple answer, which required special relativity and quantum mechanics, both used in ways that were scarcely understood at the time. When he reported his experimental and theoretical results at meetings of The American Physical Society, Compton stimulated strong interest and strong opposition. But his work quickly triumphed and had a powerful effect on the development of quantum theory. Compton's work, along with the work of others of his generation, marks the emergence of American theoretical physics as the equal of any in the world.

In 1923 Compton took up the professorship at the University of Chicago just vacated by Millikan. Like his predecessor he proved to be a remarkable teacher, attracting and stimulating many students. With their help he continued to produce important papers, first on X-rays and later on cosmic rays. Following the family tradition of Christian service to education, just after the Second World War he reluctantly left physics research to become a highly successful chancellor of Washington University.

During the war Compton was in charge of the "Metallurgical Laboratory" in Chicago where Enrico Fermi and others worked on the fission chain reaction. Leading the Met Lab was a nerve-wracking job, for the scientists there were under intense pressure. They were never sure that German scientists would not be the first to set off a nuclear bomb. Compton and many others had always felt that physics was important to the future of the nation, but this was the first time American physicists had seen that their very lives and freedom might depend on the progress of their research. When the world's first nuclear reactor went critical at the Met Lab on December 2, 1942, physicists became central figures in a new geopolitics.

Momentous though the development of the chain reaction may be, the development of atomic physics and quantum mechanics may turn out in the long run to be still more important. Compton's crucial contribution to this is laid out in the following paper, reproduced from the *Physical Review* (vol. 21, 1923, p. 483-502).

ARTHUR HOLLY COMPTON

Second Series   *May, 1923*   *Vol. 21, No. 5*

THE
PHYSICAL REVIEW

A QUANTUM THEORY OF THE SCATTERING OF X–RAYS BY LIGHT ELEMENTS

By Arthur H. Compton

Abstract

A quantum theory of the scattering of X-rays and γ-rays by light elements.
—The hypothesis is suggested that when an X-ray quantum is scattered it
spends all of its energy and momentum upon some particular electron. This
electron in turn scatters the ray in some definite direction. The change in
momentum of the X-ray quantum due to the change in its direction of propagation results in a recoil of the scattering electron. The energy in the scattered
quantum is thus less than the energy in the primary quantum by the kinetic
energy of recoil of the scattering electron. The corresponding *increase in the
wave-length of the scattered beam* is $\lambda_\theta - \lambda_0 = (2h/mc)\sin^2\frac{1}{2}\theta = 0.0484\sin^2\frac{1}{2}\theta$,
where h is the Planck constant, m is the mass of the scattering electron, c is
the velocity of light, and θ is the angle between the incident and the scattered
ray. Hence the increase is independent of the wave-length. *The distribution
of the scattered radiation* is found, by an indirect and not quite rigid method,
to be concentrated in the forward direction according to a definite law (Eq. 27).
The total energy removed from the primary beam comes out less than that given
by the classical Thomson theory in the ratio $1/(1 + 2\alpha)$, where $\alpha = h/mc\lambda_0$
$= 0.0242/\lambda_0$. Of this energy a fraction $(1 + \alpha)/(1 + 2\alpha)$ reappears as
scattered radiation, while the remainder is truly absorbed and transformed
into kinetic energy of recoil of the scattering electrons. Hence, if σ_0 is the
scattering absorption coefficient according to the classical theory, the coefficient
according to this theory is $\sigma = \sigma_0/(1 + 2\alpha) = \sigma_s + \sigma_a$, where σ_s is the true
scattering coefficient $[(1 + \alpha)\sigma/(1 + 2\alpha)^2]$, and σ_a is the coefficient of absorption due to scattering $[\alpha\sigma/(1 + 2\alpha)^2]$. Unpublished experimental results are
given which show that for graphite and the Mo–K radiation the scattered
radiation is longer than the primary, the observed difference $(\lambda_{\pi/2} - \lambda_0 = .022)$
being close to the computed value .024. In the case of scattered γ-rays, the
wave-length has been found to vary with θ in agreement with the theory,
increasing from .022 A (primary) to .068 A $(\theta = 135°)$. Also the velocity of
secondary β-rays excited in light elements by γ-rays agrees with the suggestion
that they are recoil electrons. As for the predicted variation of absorption
with λ, Hewlett's results for carbon for wave-lengths below 0.5 A are in
excellent agreement with this theory; also the predicted concentration in the
forward direction is shown to be in agreement with the experimental results,

both for X-rays and γ-rays. This remarkable *agreement between experiment and theory* indicates clearly that scattering is a quantum phenomenon and can be explained without introducing any new hypothesis as to the size of the electron or any new constants; also that a radiation quantum carries with it momentum as well as energy. The restriction to light elements is due to the assumption that the constraining forces acting on the scattering electrons are negligible, which is probably legitimate only for the lighter elements.

Spectrum of K-rays from Mo scattered by graphite, as compared with the spectrum of the primary rays, is given in Fig. 4, showing the change of wave-length.

Radiation from a moving isotropic radiator.—It is found that in a direction θ with the velocity, $I_\theta/I' = (1 - \beta)^2/(1 - \beta \cos \theta)^4 = (\nu_\theta/\nu')^4$. For the total radiation from a black body in motion to an observer at rest, $I/I' = (T/T')^4 = (\nu_m/\nu_m')^4$, where the primed quantities refer to the body at rest.

J. J. Thomson's classical theory of the scattering of X-rays, though supported by the early experiments of Barkla and others, has been found incapable of explaining many of the more recent experiments. This theory, based upon the usual electrodynamics, leads to the result that the energy scattered by an electron traversed by an X-ray beam of unit intensity is the same whatever may be the wave-length of the incident rays. Moreover, when the X-rays traverse a thin layer of matter, the intensity of the scattered radiation on the two sides of the layer should be the same. Experiments on the scattering of X-rays by light elements have shown that these predictions are correct when X-rays of moderate hardness are employed; but when very hard X-rays or γ-rays are employed, the scattered energy is found to be decidedly less than Thomson's theoretical value, and to be strongly concentrated on the emergent side of the scattering plate.

Several years ago the writer suggested that this reduced scattering of the very short wave-length X-rays might be the result of interference between the rays scattered by different parts of the electron, if the electron's diameter is comparable with the wave-length of the radiation. By assuming the proper radius for the electron, this hypothesis supplied a quantitative explanation of the scattering for any particular wave-length. But recent experiments have shown that the size of the electron which must thus be assumed increases with the wave-length of the X-rays employed,[1] and the conception of an electron whose size varies with the wave-length of the incident rays is difficult to defend.

Recently an even more serious difficulty with the classical theory of X-ray scattering has appeared. It has long been known that secondary γ-rays are softer than the primary rays which excite them, and recent experiments have shown that this is also true of X-rays. By a spectro-scopic examination of the secondary X-rays from graphite, I have, indeed,

[1] A. H. Compton, Bull. Nat. Research Council, No. 20, p. 10 (Oct., 1922).

been able to show that only a small part, if any, of the secondary X-radiation is of the same wave-length as the primary.[1] While the energy of the secondary X-radiation is so nearly equal to that calculated from Thomson's classical theory that it is difficult to attribute it to anything other than true scattering,[2] these results show that if there is any scattering comparable in magnitude with that predicted by Thomson, it is of a greater wave-length than the primary X-rays.

Such a change in wave-length is directly counter to Thomson's theory of scattering, for this demands that the scattering electrons, radiating as they do because of their forced vibrations when traversed by a primary X-ray, shall give rise to radiation of exactly the same frequency as that of the radiation falling upon them. Nor does any modification of the theory such as the hypothesis of a large electron suggest a way out of the difficulty. This failure makes it appear improbable that a satisfactory explanation of the scattering of X-rays can be reached on the basis of the classical electrodynamics.

THE QUANTUM HYPOTHESIS OF SCATTERING

According to the classical theory, each X-ray affects every electron in the matter traversed, and the scattering observed is that due to the combined effects of all the electrons. From the point of view of the quantum theory, we may suppose that any particular quantum of X-rays is not scattered by all the electrons in the radiator, but spends all of its energy upon some particular electron. This electron will in turn scatter the ray in some definite direction, at an angle with the incident beam. This bending of the path of the quantum of radiation results in a change in its momentum. As a consequence, the scattering electron will recoil with a momentum equal to the change in momentum of the X-ray. The energy in the scattered ray will be equal to that in the incident ray minus the kinetic energy of the recoil of the scattering electron; and since the scattered ray must be a complete quantum, the frequency will be reduced in the same ratio as is the energy. Thus on the quantum theory we should expect the wave-length of the scattered X-rays to be greater than that of the incident rays.

The effect of the momentum of the X-ray quantum is to set the

---

[1] In previous papers (Phil. Mag. **41**, 749, 1921; Phys. Rev. **18**, 96, 1921) I have defended the view that the softening of the secondary X-radiation was due to a considerable admixture of a form of fluorescent radiation. Gray (Phil. Mag. **26**, 611, 1913; Frank. Inst. Journ., Nov., 1920, p. 643) and Florance (Phil. Mag. **27**, 225, 1914) have considered that the evidence favored true scattering, and that the softening is in some way an accompaniment of the scattering process. The considerations brought forward in the present paper indicate that the latter view is the correct one.

[2] A. H. Compton, loc. cit., p. 16.

154

ARTHUR HOLLY COMPTON

scattering electron in motion at an angle of less than 90° with the primary beam. But it is well known that the energy radiated by a moving body is greater in the direction of its motion. We should therefore expect, as is experimentally observed, that the intensity of the scattered radiation should be greater in the general direction of the primary X-rays than in the reverse direction.

The change in wave-length due to scattering.—Imagine, as in Fig. 1*A*,

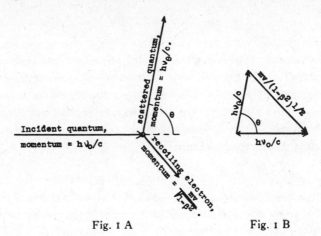

Fig. 1 A   Fig. 1 B

that an X-ray quantum of frequency ν_0 is scattered by an electron of mass m. The momentum of the incident ray will be $h\nu_0/c$, where c is the velocity of light and h is Planck's constant, and that of the scattered ray is $h\nu_\theta/c$ at an angle θ with the initial momentum. The principle of the conservation of momentum accordingly demands that the momentum of recoil of the scattering electron shall equal the vector difference between the momenta of these two rays, as in Fig. 1*B*. The momentum of the electron, $m\beta c/\sqrt{1-\beta^2}$, is thus given by the relation

$$\left(\frac{m\beta c}{\sqrt{1-\beta^2}}\right)^2 = \left(\frac{h\nu_0}{c}\right)^2 + \left(\frac{h\nu_\theta}{c}\right)^2 + 2\frac{h\nu_0}{c}\cdot\frac{h\nu_\theta}{c}\cos\theta, \qquad (1)$$

where β is the ratio of the velocity of recoil of the electron to the velocity of light. But the energy $h\nu_\theta$ in the scattered quantum is equal to that of the incident quantum $h\nu_0$ less the kinetic energy of recoil of the scattering electron, *i.e.*,

$$h\nu_\theta = h\nu_0 - mc^2\left(\frac{1}{\sqrt{1-\beta^2}} - 1\right). \qquad (2)$$

We thus have two independent equations containing the two unknown quantities β and ν_θ. On solving the equations we find

$$\nu_\theta = \nu_0/(1 + 2\alpha\sin^2\tfrac{1}{2}\theta), \qquad (3)$$

155

where

$$\alpha = h\nu_0/mc^2 = h/mc\lambda_0. \tag{4}$$

Or in terms of wave-length instead of frequency,

$$\lambda_\theta = \lambda_0 + (2h/mc)\sin^2 \tfrac{1}{2}\theta. \tag{5}$$

It follows from Eq. (2) that $1/(1 - \beta^2) = \{1 + \alpha[1 - (\nu_\theta/\nu_0)]\}^2$, or solving explicitly for β

$$\beta = 2\alpha \sin \tfrac{1}{2}\theta \, \frac{\sqrt{1 + (2\alpha + \alpha^2)\sin^2 \tfrac{1}{2}\theta}}{1 + 2(\alpha + \alpha^2)\sin^2 \tfrac{1}{2}\theta}. \tag{6}$$

Eq. (5) indicates an increase in wave-length due to the scattering process which varies from a few per cent in the case of ordinary X-rays to more than 200 per cent in the case of γ-rays scattered backward. At the same time the velocity of the recoil of the scattering electron, as calculated from Eq. (6), varies from zero when the ray is scattered directly forward to about 80 per cent of the speed of light when a γ-ray is scattered at a large angle.

It is of interest to notice that according to the classical theory, if an X-ray were scattered by an electron moving in the direction of propagation at a velocity $\beta'c$, the frequency of the ray scattered at an angle θ is given by the Doppler principle as

$$\nu_\theta = \nu_0 \bigg/ \left(1 + \frac{2\beta'}{1 - \beta'}\sin^2 \tfrac{1}{2}\theta\right). \tag{7}$$

It will be seen that this is of exactly the same form as Eq. (3), derived on the hypothesis of the recoil of the scattering electron. Indeed, if $\alpha = \beta'/(1 - \beta')$ or $\beta' = \alpha/(1 + \alpha)$, the two expressions become identical. It is clear, therefore, that so far as the effect on the wave-length is concerned, we may replace the recoiling electron by a scattering electron moving in the direction of the incident beam at a velocity such that

$$\bar\beta = \alpha/(1 + \alpha). \tag{8}$$

We shall call $\bar\beta c$ the "effective velocity" of the scattering electrons.

Energy distribution from a moving, isotropic radiator.—In preparation for the investigation of the spatial distribution of the energy scattered by a recoiling electron, let us study the energy radiated from a moving, isotropic body. If an observer moving with the radiating body draws a sphere about it, the condition of isotropy means that the probability is equal for all directions of emission of each energy quantum. That is, the probability that a quantum will traverse the sphere between the angles θ' and $\theta' + d\theta'$ with the direction of motion is $\tfrac{1}{2}\sin\theta' d\theta'$. But

ARTHUR HOLLY COMPTON

the surface which the moving observer considers a sphere (Fig. 2A) is

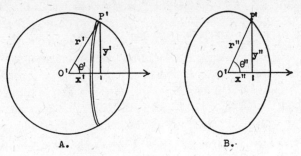

A.   B.

Fig. 2

considered by the stationary observer to be an oblate spheroid whose polar axis is reduced by the factor $\sqrt{1 - \beta^2}$. Consequently a quantum of radiation which traverses the sphere at the angle θ', whose tangent is y'/x' (Fig. 2A), appears to the stationary observer to traverse the spheroid at an angle θ'' whose tangent is y''/x'' (Fig. 2B). Since $x' = x''/\sqrt{1 - \beta^2}$ and $y' = y''$, we have

$$\tan \theta' = y'/x' = \sqrt{1 - \beta^2}\, y''/x'' = \sqrt{1 - \beta^2} \tan \theta'', \qquad (9)$$

and

$$\sin \theta' = \frac{\sqrt{1 - \beta^2}\, \tan \theta''}{\sqrt{1 + (1 - \beta^2) \tan^2 \theta''}}. \qquad (10)$$

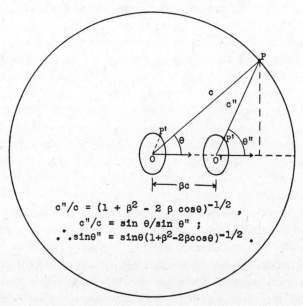

$$c''/c = (1 + \beta^2 - 2\beta \cos\theta)^{-1/2},$$
$$c''/c = \sin\theta/\sin\theta'' ;$$
$$\therefore \sin\theta'' = \sin\theta(1+\beta^2-2\beta\cos\theta)^{-1/2}.$$

Fig. 3.   The ray traversing the moving spheroid at P' at an angle θ'' reaches the stationary spherical surface drawn about O, at the point P, at an angle θ.

Imagine, as in Fig. 3, that a quantum is emitted at the instant $t = 0$, when the radiating body is at O. If it traverses the moving observer's sphere at an angle θ', it traverses the corresponding oblate spheroid, imagined by the stationary observer to be moving with the body, at an angle θ''. After 1 second, the quantum will have reached some point P on a sphere of radius c drawn about O, while the radiator will have moved a distance βc. The stationary observer at P therefore finds that the radiation is coming to him from the point O, at an angle θ with the direction of motion. That is, if the moving observer considers the quantum to be emitted at an angle θ' with the direction of motion, to the stationary observer the angle appears to be θ, where

$$\sin \theta / \sqrt{1 + \beta^2 - 2\beta \cos \theta} = \sin \theta'', \tag{11}$$

and θ'' is given in terms of θ' by Eq. (10). It follows that

$$\sin \theta' = \sin \theta \frac{\sqrt{1 - \beta^2}}{1 - \beta \cos \theta}. \tag{12}$$

On differentiating Eq. (12) we obtain

$$d\theta' = \frac{\sqrt{1 - \beta^2}}{1 - \beta \cos \theta} d\theta. \tag{13}$$

The probability that a given quantum will appear to the stationary observer to be emitted between the angles θ and $\theta + d\theta$ is therefore

$$P_\theta d\theta = P_{\theta'} d\theta' = \tfrac{1}{2} \sin \theta' d\theta',$$

where the values of $\sin \theta'$ and $d\theta'$ are given by Eqs. (12) and (13). Substituting these values we find

$$P_\theta d\theta = \frac{1 - \beta^2}{(1 - \beta \cos \theta)^2} \cdot \tfrac{1}{2} \sin \theta d\theta. \tag{14}$$

Suppose the moving observer notices that n' quanta are emitted per second. The stationary observer will estimate the rate of emission as

$$n'' = n' \sqrt{1 - \beta^2},$$

quanta per second, because of the difference in rate of the moving and stationary clocks. Of these n'' quanta, the number which are emitted between angles θ and $\theta + d\theta$ is $dn'' = n'' \cdot P_\theta d\theta$. But if dn'' per second are emitted at the angle θ, the number per second received by a stationary observer at this angle is $dn = dn''/(1 - \beta \cos \theta)$, since the radiator is approaching the observer at a velocity $\beta \cos \theta$. The energy of each quantum is, however, $h\nu_\theta$, where ν_θ is the frequency of the radiation as received by the stationary observer.[1] Thus the intensity, or the energy per unit area per unit time, of the radiation received at an angle θ and a distance R is

$$I_\theta = \frac{h\nu_\theta \cdot dn}{2\pi R^2 \sin\theta d\theta} = \frac{h\nu_\theta}{2\pi R^2 \sin\theta d\theta} \frac{n'(1-\beta^2)^{3/2}}{(1-\beta\cos\theta)^3} \tfrac{1}{2}\sin\theta d\theta$$

$$= \frac{n'h\nu_\theta}{4\pi R^2} \frac{(1-\beta^2)^{3/2}}{(1-\beta\cos\theta)^3}. \tag{15}$$

If the frequency of the oscillator emitting the radiation is measured by an observer moving with the radiator as ν', the stationary observer judges its frequency to be $\nu'' = \nu'\sqrt{1-\beta^2}$, and, in virtue of the Doppler effect, the frequency of the radiation received at an angle θ is

$$\nu_\theta = \nu''/(1-\beta\cos\theta) = \nu'[\sqrt{1-\beta^2}/(1-\beta\cos\theta)]. \tag{16}$$

Substituting this value of ν_θ in Eq. (15) we find

$$I_\theta = \frac{n'h\nu'}{4\pi R^2} \frac{(1-\beta^2)^2}{(1-\beta\cos\theta)^4}. \tag{17}$$

But the intensity of the radiation observed by the moving observer at a distance R from the source is $I' = n'h\nu'/4\pi R^2$. Thus,

$$I_\theta = I'[(1-\beta)^2/(1-\beta\cos\theta)^4] \tag{18}$$

is the intensity of the radiation received at an angle θ with the direction of motion of an isotropic radiator, which moves with a velocity βc, and which would radiate with intensity I' if it were at rest.[2]

It is interesting to note, on comparing Eqs. (16) and (18), that

$$I_\theta/I' = (\nu_\theta/\nu')^4. \tag{19}$$

[1] At first sight the assumption that the quantum which to the moving observer had energy $h\nu'$ will be $h\nu$ for the stationary observer seems inconsistent with the energy principle. When one considers, however, the work done by the moving body against the back-pressure of the radiation, it is found that the energy principle is satisfied. The conclusion reached by the present method of calculation is in exact accord with that which would be obtained according to Lorenz's equations, by considering the radiation to consist of electromagnetic waves.

[2] G. H. Livens gives for I_θ/I' the value $(1-\beta\cos\theta)^{-2}$ ("The Theory of Electricity," p. 600, 1918). At small velocities this value differs from the one here obtained by the factor $(1-\beta\cos\theta)^{-2}$. The difference is due to Livens' neglect of the concentration of the radiation in the small angles, as expressed by our Eq. (14). Cunningham ("The Principle of Relativity," p. 60, 1914) shows that if a plane wave is emitted by a radiator moving in the direction of propagation with a velocity βc, the intensity I received by a stationary observer is greater than the intensity I' estimated by the moving observer, in the ratio $(1-\beta^2)/(1-\beta)^2$, which is in accord with the value calculated according to the methods here employed.

The change in frequency given in Eq. (16) is that of the usual relativity theory. I have not noticed the publication of any result which is the equivalent of my formula (18) for the intensity of the radiation from a moving body.

159

ARTHUR HOLLY COMPTON

This result may be obtained very simply for the total radiation from a black body, which is a special case of an isotropic radiator. For, suppose such a radiator is moving so that the frequency of maximum intensity which to a moving observer is ν_m' appears to the stationary observer to be ν_m. Then according to Wien's law, the apparent temperature T, as estimated by the stationary observer, is greater than the temperature T' for the moving observer by the ratio $T/T' = \nu_m/\nu_m'$. According to Stefan's law, however, the intensity of the total radiation from a black body is proportional to T^4; hence, if I and I' are the intensities of the radiation as measured by the stationary and the moving observers respectively,

$$I/I' = (T/T')^4 = (\nu_m/\nu_m')^4. \tag{20}$$

The agreement of this result with Eq. (19) may be taken as confirming the correctness of the latter expression.

The intensity of scattering from recoiling electrons.—We have seen that the change in frequency of the radiation scattered by the recoiling electrons is the same as if the radiation were scattered by electrons moving in the direction of propagation with an effective velocity $\bar{\beta} = \alpha/(1 + \alpha)$, where $\alpha = h/mc\lambda_0$. It seems obvious that since these two methods of calculation result in the same change in wave-length, they must also result in the same change in intensity of the scattered beam. This assumption is supported by the fact that we find, as in Eq. 19, that the change in intensity is in certain special cases a function only of the change in frequency. I have not, however, succeeded in showing rigidly that if two methods of scattering result in the same relative wave-lengths at different angles, they will also result in the same relative intensity at different angles. Nevertheless, we shall assume that this proposition is true, and shall proceed to calculate the relative intensity of the scattered beam at different angles on the hypothesis that the scattering electrons are moving in the direction of the primary beam with a velocity $\bar{\beta} = \alpha/(1 + \alpha)$. If our assumption is correct, the results of the calculation will apply also to the scattering by recoiling electrons.

To an observer moving with the scattering electron, the intensity of the scattering at an angle θ', according to the usual electrodynamics, should be proportional to $(1 + \cos^2 \theta')$, if the primary beam is unpolarized. On the quantum theory, this means that the probability that a quantum will be emitted between the angles θ' and $\theta' + d\theta'$ is proportional to $(1 + \cos^2 \theta') \cdot \sin \theta' d\theta'$, since $2\pi \sin \theta' d\theta'$ is the solid angle included between θ' and $\theta' + d\theta'$. This may be written $P_{\theta'} d\theta' = k(1 + \cos^2 \theta') \sin \theta' d\theta'$.

33

The factor of proportionality k may be determined by performing the integration

$$\int_0^\pi P_{\theta'}d\theta' = k \int_0^\pi (1 + \cos^2 \theta') \sin \theta'd\theta' = 1,$$

with the result that $k = 3/8$. Thus

$$P_{\theta'}d\theta' = (3/8)(1 + \cos^2 \theta') \sin \theta'd\theta' \qquad (21)$$

is the probability that a quantum will be emitted at the angle θ' as measured by an observer moving with the scattering electron.

To the stationary observer, however, the quantum ejected at an angle θ' appears to move at an angle θ with the direction of the primary beam, where $\sin \theta'$ and $d\theta'$ are as given in Eqs. (12) and (13). Substituting these values in Eq. (21), we find for the probability that a given quantum will be scattered between the angles θ and $\theta + d\theta$,

$$P_\theta d\theta = \tfrac{3}{8} \sin \theta d\theta \frac{(1 - \beta^2)\{(1 + \beta^2)(1 + \cos^2 \theta) - 4\beta \cos \theta\}}{(1 - \beta \cos \theta)^4}. \qquad (22)$$

Suppose the stationary observer notices that n quanta are scattered per second. In the case of the radiator emitting n'' quanta per second while approaching the observer, the n''th quantum was emitted when the radiator was nearer the observer, so that the interval between the receipt of the 1st and the n''th quantum was less than a second. That is, more quanta were received per second than were emitted in the same time. In the case of scattering, however, though we suppose that each scattering electron is moving forward, the nth quantum is scattered by an electron starting from the same position as the 1st quantum. Thus the number of quanta received per second is also n.

We have seen (Eq. 3) that the frequency of the quantum received at an angle θ is $\nu_\theta = \nu_0/(1 + 2\alpha \sin^2 \tfrac{1}{2}\theta) = \nu_0/\{1 + \alpha(1 - \cos \theta)\}$, where ν_0, the frequency of the incident beam, is also the frequency of the ray scattered in the direction of the incident beam. The energy scattered per second at the angle θ is thus $nh\nu_\theta P_\theta d\theta$, and the intensity, or energy per second per unit area, of the ray scattered to a distance R is

$$I_\theta = \frac{nh\nu_\theta P_\theta d\theta}{2\pi R^2 \sin \theta d\theta}$$

$$= \frac{nh}{2\pi R^2} \cdot \frac{\nu_0}{1 + \alpha(1 - \cos \theta)} \cdot \frac{3}{8} \cdot \frac{(1 - \beta^2)\{(1 + \beta^2)(1 + \cos^2 \theta) - 4\beta \cos \theta\}}{(1 - \beta \cos \theta)^4}.$$

Substituting for β its value $\alpha/(1 + \alpha)$, and reducing, this becomes

$$I = \frac{3nh\nu_0}{16\pi R} \frac{(1 + 2\alpha)\{1 + \cos^2 \theta + 2\alpha(1 + \alpha)(1 - \cos \theta)^2\}}{(1 + \alpha - \alpha \cos \theta)^5}. \qquad (23)$$

161

ARTHUR HOLLY COMPTON

In the forward direction, where $\theta = 0$, the intensity of the scattered beam is thus

$$I_0 = \frac{3}{8\pi} \frac{nh\nu_0}{R^2} (1 + 2\alpha). \tag{24}$$

Hence

$$\frac{I_\theta}{I_0} = \frac{1}{2} \frac{1 + \cos^2 \theta + 2\alpha(1 + \alpha)(1 - \cos \theta)^2}{\{1 + \alpha(1 - \cos \theta)\}^5}. \tag{25}$$

On the hypothesis of recoiling electrons, however, for a ray scattered directly forward, the velocity of recoil is zero (Eq. 6). Since in this case the scattering electron is at rest, the intensity of the scattered beam should be that calculated on the basis of the classical theory, namely,

$$I_0 = I(Ne^4/R^2m^2c^4), \tag{26}$$

where I is the intensity of the primary beam traversing the N electrons which are effective in scattering. On combining this result with Eq. (25), we find for the intensity of the X-rays scattered at an angle θ with the incident beam,

$$I = I \frac{Ne^4}{2R^2m^2c^4} \frac{1 + \cos^2 \theta + 2\alpha(1 + \alpha)(1 - \cos \theta)^2}{\{1 + \alpha(1 - \cos \theta)\}^5}. \tag{27}$$

The calculation of the energy removed from the primary beam may now be made without difficulty. We have supposed that n quanta are scattered per second. But on comparing Eqs. (24) and (26), we find that

$$n = \frac{8\pi}{3} \frac{INe^4}{h\nu_0 m^2 c^4 (1 + 2\alpha)}.$$

The energy removed from the primary beam per second is $nh\nu_0$. If we define *the scattering absorption coefficient* as the fraction of the energy of the primary beam removed by the scattering process per unit length of path through the medium, it has the value

$$\sigma = \frac{nh\nu_0}{I} = \frac{8\pi}{3} \frac{Ne^4}{m^2c^4} \cdot \frac{1}{1 + 2\alpha} = \frac{\sigma_0}{1 + 2\alpha}, \tag{28}$$

where N is the number of scattering electrons per unit volume, and σ_0 is the scattering coefficient calculated on the basis of the classical theory.[1]

In order to determine the total energy truly scattered, we must integrate the scattered intensity over the surface of a sphere surrounding the scattering material, *i.e.*, $\epsilon_s = \int_0^\pi I_\theta \cdot 2\pi R^2 \sin \theta d\theta$. On substituting the value of I_θ from Eq. (27), and integrating, this becomes

$$\epsilon_s = \frac{8\pi}{3} \frac{INe^4}{m^2c^4} \frac{1 + \alpha}{(1 + 2\alpha)^2}.$$

[1] Cf. J. J. Thomson, "Conduction of Electricity through Gases," 2d ed., p. 325.

162

ARTHUR HOLLY COMPTON

The *true scattering coefficient* is thus

$$\sigma_s = \frac{8\pi}{3}\frac{Ne^4}{m^2c^4}\frac{1+\alpha}{(1+2\alpha)^2} = \sigma_0\frac{1+\alpha}{(1+2\alpha)^2}. \tag{29}$$

It is clear that the difference between the total energy removed from the primary beam and that which reappears as scattered radiation is the energy of recoil of the scattering electrons. This difference represents, therefore, a type of true absorption resulting from the scattering process. The corresponding *coefficient of true absorption due to scattering* is

$$\sigma_a = \sigma - \sigma_s = \frac{8\pi}{3}\frac{Ne^4}{m^2c^4}\frac{\alpha}{(1+2\alpha)^2} = \sigma_0\frac{\alpha}{(1+2\alpha)^2}. \tag{30}$$

Experimental Test.

Let us now investigate the agreement of these various formulas with exper ments on the change of wave-length due to scattering, and on the magnitude of the scattering of X-rays and γ-rays by light elements.

Wave-length of the scattered rays.—If in Eq. (5) we substitute the accepted values of h, m, and c, we obtain

$$\lambda_\theta = \lambda_0 + 0.0484 \sin^2 \tfrac{1}{2}\theta, \tag{31}$$

if λ is expressed in Angström units. It is perhaps surprising that the increase should be the same for all wave-lengths. Yet, as a result of an extensive experimental study of the change in wave-length on scattering, the writer has concluded that "over the range of primary rays from 0.7 to 0.025 A, the wave-length of the secondary X-rays at 90° with the incident beam is roughly 0.03 A greater than that of the primary beam which excites it." [1] Thus the experiments support the theory in showing a wave-length increase which seems independent of the incident wave-length, and which also is of the proper order of magnitude.

A quantitative test of the accuracy of Eq. (31) is possible in the case of the characteristic K-rays from molybdenum when scattered by graphite. In Fig. 4 is shown a spectrum of the X-rays scattered by graphite at right angles with the primary beam, when the graphite is traversed by X-rays from a molybdenum target.[2] The solid line represents the spectrum of these scattered rays, and is to be compared with the broken line, which represents the spectrum of the primary rays, using the same slits and crystal, and the same potential on the tube. The primary spectrum is, of course, plotted on a much smaller scale than

[1] A. H. Compton, Bull. N. R. C., No. 20, p. 17 (1922)

[2] It is hoped to publish soon a description of the experiments on which this figure is based.

the secondary. The zero point for the spectrum of both the primary and secondary X-rays was determined by finding the position of the first order lines on both sides of the zero point.

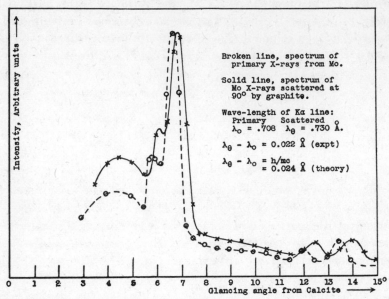

Fig. 4. Spectrum of molybdenum X-rays scattered by graphite, compared with the spectrum of the primary X-rays, showing an increase in wave-length on scattering.

It will be seen that the wave-length of the scattered rays is unquestionably, greater than that of the primary rays which excite them. Thus the $K\alpha$ line from molybdenum has a wave-length 0.708 A. The wave-length of this line in the scattered beam is found in these experiments, however, to be 0.730 A. That is,

$$\lambda_\theta - \lambda_0 = 0.022 \text{ A} \quad \text{(experiment)}.$$

But according to the present theory (Eq. 5),

$$\lambda_\theta - \lambda_0 = 0.0484 \sin^2 45° = 0.024 \text{ A} \quad \text{(theory)},$$

which is a very satisfactory agreement.

The variation in wave-length of the scattered beam with the angle is illustrated in the case of γ-rays. The writer has measured [1] the mass absorption coefficient in lead of the rays scattered at different angles when various substances are traversed by the hard γ-rays from RaC. The mean results for iron, aluminium and paraffin are given in column 2 of Table I. This variation in absorption coefficient corresponds to a

[1] A. H. Compton, Phil. Mag. **41**, 760 (1921).

difference in wave-length at the different angles. Using the value given by Hull and Rice for the mass absorption coefficient in lead for wave-length 0.122, 3.0, remembering [1] that the characteristic fluorescent absorption τ/ρ is proportional to λ^3, and estimating the part of the absorption due to scattering by the method described below, I find for the wave-lengths corresponding to these absorption coefficients the values given in the fourth column of Table I. That this extrapolation is very

TABLE I

Wave-length of Primary and Scattered γ-rays

	Angle	μ/ρ	τ/ρ	λ obs.	λ calc.
Primary.......	0°	.076	.017	0.022 A	(0.022 A)
Scattered.....	45°	.10	.042	.030	0.029
"	90°	.21	.123	.043	0.047
"	135°	.59	.502	.668	0.063

nearly correct is indicated by the fact that it gives for the primary beam a wave-length 0.022 A. This is in good accord with the writer's value 0.025 A, calculated from the scattering of γ-rays by lead at small angles,[2] and with Ellis' measurements from his β-ray spectra, showing lines of wave-length .045, .025, .021 and .020 A, with line .020 the strongest.[3] Taking $\lambda_0 = 0.022$ A, the wave-lengths at the other angles may be calculated from Eq. (31). The results, given in the last column of Table I., and shown graphically in Fig. 5, are in satisfactory accord with the measured values. There is thus good reason for believing that Eq. (5) represents accurately the wave-length of the X-rays and γ-rays scattered by light elements.

Velocity of recoil of the scattering electrons.—The electrons which recoil in the process of the scattering of ordinary X-rays have not been observed. This is probably because their number and velocity is usually small compared with the number and velocity of the photoelectrons ejected as a result of the characteristic fluorescent absorption. I have pointed out elsewhere,[4] however, that there is good reason for believing that most of the secondary β-rays excited in light elements by the action of γ-rays are such recoil electrons. According to Eq. (6), the velocity of these electrons should vary from 0, when the γ-ray is scattered forward, to $v_{max} = \beta_{max}c = 2c\alpha[(1 + \alpha)/(1 + 2\alpha + 2\alpha^2)]$, when the γ-ray quantum

[1] Cf. L. de Broglie, Jour. de Phys. et Rad. **3**, 33 (1922); A. H. Compton, Bull. N. R. C., No. 20, p. 43 (1922).

[2] A. H. Compton, Phil. Mag. **41**, 777 (1921).

[3] C. D. Ellis, Proc. Roy. Soc. A, **101**, 6 (1922).

[4] A. H. Compton, Bull. N. R. C., No. 20, p. 27 (1922).

is scattered backward. If for the hard γ-rays from radium C, $\alpha = 1.09$, corresponding to $\lambda = 0.022$ A, we thus obtain $\beta_{max} = 0.82$. The effective velocity of the scattering electrons is, therefore (Eq. 8), $\bar{\beta} = 0.52$. These results are in accord with the fact that the average velocity of the

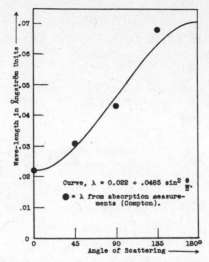

Fig. 5. The wave-length of scattered γ-rays at different angles with the primary beam, showing an increase at large angles similar to a Doppler effect.

β-rays excited by the γ-rays from radium is somewhat greater than half that of light.[1]

Absorption of X-rays due to scattering.—Valuable information concerning the magnitude of the scattering is given by the measurements of the absorption of X-rays due to scattering. Over a wide range of wave-lengths, the formula for the total mass absorption, $\mu/\rho = \kappa\lambda^3 + \sigma/\rho$, is found to hold, where μ is the linear absorption coefficient, ρ is the density, κ is a constant, and σ is the energy loss due to the scattering process. Usually the term $\kappa\lambda^3$, which represents the fluorescent absorption, is the more important; but when light elements and short wave-lengths are employed, the scattering process accounts for nearly all the energy loss. In this case, the constant κ can be determined by measurements on the longer wave-lengths, and the value of σ/ρ can then be estimated with considerable accuracy for the shorter wave-lengths from the observed values of μ/ρ.

Hewlett has measured the total absorption coefficient for carbon over a wide range of wave-lengths.[2] From his data for the longer wave-

---

[1] E. Rutherford, Radioactive Substances and their Radiations, p. 273.

[2] C. W. Hewlett, Phys. Rev. **17**, 284 (1921).

lengths I estimate the value of κ to be 0.912, if λ is expressed in A.   On subtracting the corresponding values of $\kappa\lambda^3$ from his observed values of μ/ρ, the values of σ/ρ represented by the crosses of Fig. 6 are obtained.

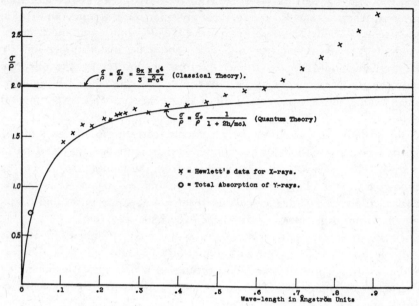

Fig. 6.   The absorption in carbon due to scattering, for homogeneous X-rays.

The value of σ_0/ρ as calculated for carbon from Thomson's formula is shown by the horizontal line at $\sigma/\rho = 0.201$.   The values of σ/ρ calculated from Eq. (28) are represented by the solid curve.   The circle shows the experimental value of the total absorption of γ-rays by carbon, which on the present view is due wholly to the scattering process.

For wave-lengths less than 0.5 A, where the test is most significant, the agreement is perhaps within the experimental error.   Experiments by Owen,[1] Crowther,[2] and Barkla and Ayers[3] show that at about 0.5 A the "excess scattering" begins to be appreciable, increasing rapidly in importance at the longer wave-lengths.[4]   It is probably this effect which results in the increase of the scattering absorption above the theoretical value for the longer wave-lengths.   Thus the experimental values of the absorption due to scattering seem to be in satisfactory accord with the present theory.

True absorption due to scattering has not been noticed in the case of

[1] E. A. Owen, Proc. Camb. Phil. Soc. **16**, 165 (1911).
[2] J. A. Crowther, Proc. Roy. Soc. **86**, 478 (1912).
[3] Barkla and Ayers, Phil. Mag. **21**, 275 (1911).
[4] Cf. A. H. Compton, Washington University Studies, **8**, 109 ff. (1921).

X-rays. In the case of hard γ-rays, however, Ishino has shown [1] that there is true absorption as well as scattering, and that for the lighter elements the true absorption is proportional to the atomic number. That is, this absorption is proportional to the number of electrons present, just as is the scattering. He gives for the true mass absorption coefficient of the hard γ-rays from RaC in both aluminium and iron the value 0.021. According to Eq. (30), the true mass absorption by aluminium should be 0.021 and by iron, 0.020, taking the effective wave-length of the rays to be 0.022 A. The difference between the theory and the experiments is less than the probable experimental error.

Ishino has also estimated the true mass scattering coefficients of the hard γ-rays from RaC by aluminium and iron to be 0.045 and 0.042 respectively.[2] These values are very far from the values 0.193 and 0.187 predicted by the classical theory. But taking $\lambda = 0.022$ A, as before, the corresponding values calculated from Eq. (29) are 0.040 and 0.038, which do not differ seriously from the experimental values.

It is well known that for soft X-rays scattered by light elements the total scattering is in accord with Thomson's formula. This is in agreement with the present theory, according to which the true scattering coefficient σ_s approaches Thomson's value σ_0 when $\alpha \equiv h/mc\lambda$ becomes small (Eq. 29).

The relative intensity of the X-rays scattered in different directions with the primary beam.—Our Eq. (27) predicts a concentration of the energy in the forward direction. A large number of experiments on the scattering of X-rays have shown that, except for the excess scattering at small angles, the ionization due to the scattered beam is symmetrical on the emergence and incidence sides of a scattering plate. The difference in intensity on the two sides according to Eq. (27) should, however, be noticeable. Thus if the wave-length is 0.7 A, which is probably about that used by Barkla and Ayers in their experiments on the scattering by carbon,[3] the ratio of the intensity of the rays scattered at 40° to that at 140° should be about 1.10. But their experimental ratio was 1.04, which differs from our theory by more than their probable experimental error.

It will be remembered, however, that our theory, and experiment also, indicates a difference in the wave-length of the X-rays scattered in different directions. The softer X-rays which are scattered backward are the more easily absorbed and, though of smaller intensity, may produce an

[1] M. Ishino, Phil. Mag. **33**, 140 (1917).

[2] M. Ishino, loc. cit.

[3] Barkla and Ayers, loc. cit.

168

ARTHUR HOLLY COMPTON

ionization equal to that of the beam scattered forward. Indeed, if α is small compared with unity, as is the case for ordinary X-rays, Eq. (27) may be written approximately $I_\theta/I_\theta' = (\lambda_0/\lambda_\theta)^3$, where I_θ' is the intensity of the beam scattered at the angle θ according to the classical theory. The part of the absorption which results in ionization is however proportional to λ^3. Hence if, as is usually the case, only a small part of the X-rays entering the ionization chamber is absorbed by the gas in the chamber, the ionization is also proportional to λ^3. Thus if i_θ represents the ionization due to the beam scattered at the angle θ, and if i_θ' is the corresponding ionization on the classical theory, we have $i_\theta/i_\theta' = (I_\theta/I_\theta')(\lambda_\theta/\lambda_0)^3 = 1$, or $i_\theta = i_\theta'$. That is, to a first approximation, the ionization should be the same as that on the classical theory, though the energy in the scattered beam is less. This conclusion is in good accord with the experiments which have been performed on the scattering of ordinary X-rays, if correction is made for the excess scattering which appears at small angles..

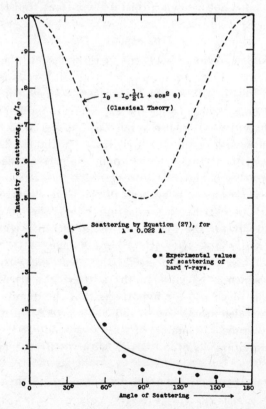

Fig. 7.   Comparison of experimental and theoretical intensities of scattered γ-rays.

ARTHUR HOLLY COMPTON

In the case of very short wave-lengths, however, the case is different. The writer has measured the γ-rays scattered at different angles by iron, using an ionization chamber so designed as to absorb the greater part of even the primary γ-ray beam.[1]   It is not clear just how the ionization due to the γ-rays will vary with the wave-length under the conditions of the experiment, but it appears probable that the variation will not be great.   If we suppose accordingly that the ionization measures the intensity of the scattered γ-ray beam, these data for the intensity are represented by the circles in Fig. 7.   The experiments showed that the intensity at 90° was 0.074 times that predicted by the classical theory, or 0.037 I_0, where I_0 is the intensity of the scattering at the angle $\theta = 0$ as calculated on either the classical or the quantum theory.   The absolute intensities of the scattered beam are accordingly plotted using I_0 as the unit.   The solid curve shows the intensity in the same units, calculated according to Eq. (27).   As before, the wave-length of the γ-rays is taken as 0.022 A.   The beautiful agreement between the theoretical and the experimental values of the scattering is the more striking when one notices that there is not a single adjustable constant connecting the two sets of values.

Discussion

This remarkable agreement between our formulas and the experiments can leave but little doubt that the scattering of X-rays is a quantum phenomenon.   The hypothesis of a large electron to explain these effects is accordingly superfluous, for all the experiments on X-ray scattering to which this hypothesis has been applied are now seen to be explicable from the point of view of the quantum theory without introducing any new hypotheses or constants.   In addition, the present theory accounts satisfactorily for the change in wave-length due to scattering, which was left unaccounted for on the hypothesis of the large electron.   From the standpoint of the scattering of X-rays and γ-rays, therefore, there is no longer any support for the hypothesis of an electron whose diameter is comparable with the wave-length of hard X-rays.

The present theory depends essentially upon the assumption that each electron which is effective in the scattering scatters a complete quantum.   It involves also the hypothesis that the quanta of radiation are received from definite directions and are scattered in definite directions.   The experimental support of the theory indicates very convincingly that a radiation quantum carries with it directed momentum as well as energy.

Emphasis has been laid upon the fact that in its present form the

[1] A. H. Compton, Phil. Mag. **41**, 758 (1921).

170

ARTHUR HOLLY COMPTON

quantum theory of scattering applies only to light elements. The reason for this restriction is that we have tacitly assumed that there are no forces of constraint acting upon the scattering electrons. This assumption is probably legitimate in the case of the very light elements, but cannot be true for the heavy elements. For if the kinetic energy of recoil of an electron is less than the energy required to remove the electron from the atom, there is no chance for the electron to recoil in the manner we have supposed. The conditions of scattering in such a case remain to be investigated.

The manner in which interference occurs, as for example in the cases of excess scattering and X-ray reflection, is not yet clear. Perhaps if an electron is bound in the atom too firmly to recoil, the incident quantum of radiation may spread itself over a large number of electrons, distributing its energy and momentum among them, thus making interference possible. In any case, the problem of scattering is so closely allied with those of reflection and interference that a study of the problem may very possibly shed some light upon the difficult question of the relation between interference and the quantum theory.

Many of the ideas involved in this paper have been developed in discussion with Professor G. E. M. Jauncey of this department.

WASHINGTON UNIVERSITY,
 SAINT LOUIS,
  December 13, 1922

Afterword:
The Last Fifty Years

It would be impossible to commemorate all the notable American physicists of the last fifty years within one volume, for there have been so many of them. Until the 1920's only two or three dozen physics Ph.D.'s were granted each year in the United States, but by the 1970's the number had risen to over a thousand per year. This exponential rise in the training of physicists was parallelled by equally steep growth in the numbers of working physicists and their production of research. The American Physical Society, which had 59 members when it was founded in 1899 and some 1800 members in 1926, had over 28,000 in 1976. The increasing population of physicists, and its diversity, were also shown by the founding of new organizations such as the Optical Society of America (1916), the Society of Rheology (1929), the Acoustical Society of America (1929), the American Association of Physics Teachers (1930), the American Crystallographic Association (1949), and the American Association of Physicists in Medicine (1958); many other physicists could be found in older groups such as the American Astronomical Society and the engineering societies. A number of these organizations became members of the American Institute of Physics, which since 1931 printed journals and managed related matters which were more efficiently done jointly.

The world economic and political catastrophes of the 1930's did not retard the growth of American physics. Despite budget problems during the Great Depression, laboratories maintained their work and welcomed physicists who emigrated from Europe and elsewhere. Albert Einstein, Enrico Fermi, and over a hundred more of the world's finest physicists found refuge in the United States. While these emigrés brought their talents, America more than any other country gave them the opportunity to use them. Even without this addition, by 1940 the United States would have been the equal in physics of any country in the world, thanks to the spectacular rise in the number and quality of native-trained people, but with the aid of the emigrés America rose to predominance. An example: When nuclear fission was discovered and many papers were published in 1939 to follow up the discovery, almost twice as many of these were published in the United States as in any other nation, a substantial number of them by refugee physicists.

The Second World War forced a pause in physics education and publication but brought an enormous leap in funding. Working on radar at the MIT Radiation Laboratory, on nuclear weapons within the huge Manhattan Project, and on other equally important research, physicists drew for the first time on the full resources of the government. In many ways their work helped to shorten the war.

Government support continued after the war. Laboratories within the federal government were nothing new—the National Bureau of Standards and others had done valuable physics research since around the turn of the century. But now government contracts, supplementing increased state and local funds and foundation grants, became a major source of support for physics laboratories. Most spectacular among these were the great new particle accelerators, mostly descended from the cyclotron laboratory that Ernest O. Lawrence had created at Berkeley, California in the 1930's. Some scientists were worried by the trend towards costly apparatus and huge, anonymous research teams, but there was no denying the high level that discovery was reaching in the United States. Of the 46 people who won a Nobel prize in physics up to 1940, only six had been American; but of the 57 winners since, 28 were American. (Five more emigrated to the United States after doing the work for which they won the prize.) No other nation in modern times has so dominated a field of science.

Less celebrated but no less important than the advance in basic science was the progress of applied physics. This was carried out particularly by people in industry, who in 1976 amounted to about a fifth of the over 20,000 Ph.D. physicists employed in the United States. Advances in applied physics profoundly affected the country's mode of life and its standing in the world economy. Also noteworthy was the progress of physics education. Before the First World War less than a tenth of American youths graduated from high school and only a small fraction of those went on to college, while in the 1970's physicists were meeting the challenge of instructing a much larger part of the population, and doing it with greatly improved curricula.

By the 1960's foresighted people were pointing out that if the exponential growth of physics was extrapolated for another two centuries, there would have to be more physicists than people in America; at some point the growth would have to level off. But it was equally clear that the science of physics had become so woven into the national life, so fundamental to American industry, defense, education and ways of thought, that it would long retain the central position it had so painstakingly won.

Sources

For further information on the physicists commemorated in this book, or indeed on any significant scientist of the past, the first thing to do is to look up their names in the *Dictionary of Scientific Biography* (1970-   ), a multi-volume reference work with the finest and most up-to-date historical scholarship. The thorough bibliographies in these articles include the sources we have used for each physicist, except for a few sources mentioned below.

The quote from Franklin's *Autobiography* is borrowed from I. Bernard Cohen's edition of Franklin's *Experiments and Observations* (1941), p. 19; further information on Franklin's work will be found in a forthcoming history of early electricity by John L. Heilbron. The letter from Henry is in Nathan Reingold, ed., *Science in Nineteenth Century America* (1964), p. 71. The Rowland trial quote was furnished by John D. Miller from his Oregon State University thesis, *Henry Augustus Rowland and his Electromagnetic Researches* (1970), p. 330; the apocryphal story is in Dorothy Michelson Livingston, *Master of Light, A Biography of Albert A. Michelson* (1973), p. 104-05, and another version is in Helen Wright, *Explorer of the Universe, A Biography of George Ellery Hale* (1966), p. 60—both excellent books. The quote about Gibbs is from Pierre Duhem, *Josiah-Willard Gibbs* (1908), p. 26, translated by the editor; the first quote by Gibbs is from the *American Journal of Science*, ser. 3, vol. 16, 1878, p. 441, while the quote from Gibbs' letter is in Martin Klein's article "Gibbs" in the *Dictionary of Scientific Biography*, vol. 5, p. 391-92. The Millikan quote is from his *Autobiography* (1950), p. 69. The advice of Compton's father is borrowed from Roger H. Stuewer, *The Compton Effect, Turning Point in Physics* (1975), p. 92. For statistics on physicists see *Historical Studies in the Physical Sciences*, vol. 5 (1975); the National Academy of Sciences report *Physics in Perspective* (1972); and reports by Beverly Porter of the Manpower Statistics Division of the American Institute of Physics.

Further information on the history of American physics can be obtained from the AIP's Center for History of Physics in New York City.

The portraits were chosen to show the physicists as they looked around the time they wrote the papers which we have reproduced. That of Franklin is a detail from a painting by Robert Feke, courtesy of the Harvard University Portrait Collection. The rest are from collections deposited at the Niels Bohr Library, AIP.